PRACTICAL
SOCIAL WORK
Series Editor: Jo Campling

[BASW]

Social work is at an important stage in its development. All professions must be responsive to changing social and economic conditions if they are to meet the needs of those they serve. This series focuses on sound practice and the specific contribution which social workers can make to the well-being of our society in the 1980s.

The British Association of Social Workers has always been conscious of its role in setting guidelines for practice and in seeking to raise professional standards. The conception of the Practical Social Work series arose from a survey of BASW members to discover where they, the practitioners in social work, felt there was the most need for new literature. The response was overwhelming and enthusiastic, and the result is a carefully planned, coherent series of books. The emphasis is firmly on practice, set in a theoretical framework. The books will inform, stimulate and promote discussion, thus adding to the further development of skills and high professional standards. All the authors are practitioners and teachers of social work, representing a wide variety of experience.

JO CAMPLING

PRACTICAL SOCIAL WORK

Series Editor: Jo Campling

BASW

EDITORIAL ADVISORY BOARD

Terry Bamford, Malcolm Payne, Peter Riches,
Sue Walrond-Skinner

PUBLISHED

Social Work and Mental Handicap
David Anderson

Social Work and Mental Illness
Alan Butler and Colin Pritchard

Residential Work
Roger Clough

Social Work with Old People
Mary Marshall

Social Work with Disabled People
Michael Oliver

Working in Teams
Malcolm Payne

Social Work with the Dying and Bereaved
Carole R. Smith

Community Work
Alan Twelvetrees

FORTHCOMING

Working with Families
Gill Gorrell-Barnes

Social Work with Ethnic Minorities
Alun Jackson

Applied Psychology for Social Workers
Paula Nicolson and Rowan Bayne

Adoption and Fostering
Carole R. Smith

Social Work with Juvenile Offenders
David Thorpe, Norman Tutt, David Smith
and Christopher Green

Social Work and Mental Illness

Alan Butler

Colin Pritchard

First published 1983 by
THE MACMILLAN PRESS LTD
London and Basingstoke
Companies and representatives throughout the world

ISBN 0 333 32704 7 (hard cover)
ISBN 0 333 32705 5 (paper cover)

Typeset in Great Britain by
CAMBRIAN TYPESETTERS
Aldershot, Hants

Printed in Hong Kong

Contents

Acknowledgements

The preparation of this book has been considerably assisted by the following people who read drafts of the different chapters: Mike Beebe, Rob Brown, Isobel Card, Mike Kerfoot, Joe Oliver and Michael Winterson. We have not always followed their suggestions and we are entirely responsible for any error or mis-statements that remain. Jo Campling and Steven Kennedy offered consistent editorial encouragement and support.

Our intellectual indebtedness will become obvious from the bibliography. But final thanks must go to the indefatigable secretarial support we received at different times from Jayne Chirouf, Joanne Compton, Val Kincaid, Pam Lyle and Agnès Pavey.

The names of people used in the case studies have been changed to preserve their anonymity.

Alan Butler
Colin Pritchard

Introduction

To many of us the mention of mental illness conjures up a picture of bizarre madness and large grim Victorian hospitals. And yet, in its varying forms, mental illness is widespread in the population and rarely fits this bleak picture. Goldberg and Huxley (1980) in a recent study of pathways to psychiatric care make it clear not only how prevalent such disorders are, with all their attendant misery, but also how many psychiatric illnesses pass unrecognised by family doctors and how small a minority of cases are referred to the psychiatric services.

Social workers in the course of their everyday work will come across many such cases of unidentified and even unacknowledged mental illness. A few social workers will specialise in the care of people who have been formally diagnosed as mentally ill. This may be either in the setting of a psychiatric hospital or based in an area team but primarily concerned with mental health after-care. However, all social workers, whatever their specialism, will encounter the psychiatrically ill among their general caseload, not infrequently at the crucial beginning of the client's breakdown. Whatever the initial referral states — it may be the threat of child abuse, or the need for re-housing — many will contain a psychiatric dimension. Most social workers can point to such people in their workload, but many remain sceptical about their ability to intervene or offer effective help in such circumstances.

The aim of this book is to provide, for the busy social-work practitioner, a practical guide to work with mentally ill people. It is *not*, however, intended to be a textbook of psychiatry. There are many of these available and reference is made to some of them in the guide to further reading, which appears towards the end of this book. For this reason we do not involve ourselves in the lengthy debate about the causes of mental illness, nor do we spend a great deal of time discussing the niceties of diagnostic classification. We believe that the social worker involved in such cases, should focus his or her attention upon the implications of the disorder for that individual and his or her family. Consequently our book is essentially about practice and we have tried to capture something of the flavour of social work with the mentally ill; to highlight the impact that such disorders may have upon the client and family and to offer some practical guides to intervention strategies. We are not unaware of the considerable debate which surrounds many aspects of contemporary psychiatric practice and have pointed to them in the text. However, we have not pursued them at great length, preferring to refer the interested reader to the appropriate literature.

The importance and centrality of mental health work has increased for the generic social worker in recent years. This is the result of a number of changes of which we mention just three. First, the Seebohm reorganisation of social work was interpreted by many to mean the demise of the specialist psychiatric social worker, although the report did in fact acknowledge the need for some specialist practice mentioning mental health work in this regard. However, in principle, the result has been that many more clients with mental health problems have found their way onto the case-loads of generic social workers. Second, we have witnessed over the last twenty years the running down of many of our larger psychiatric institutions as the emphasis has moved to further care in the community. This too has meant that more people suffering from psychiatric disorders have come into the ambit of the area-based social worker. Finally, the 1982 Amendments to the Mental Health Act of 1959 reassert the role to be played by social work in the care of those who are psychiatrically disordered.

It is against this background that we saw the need for a basic introduction to social work with mentally ill people.

One of our central themes is that for a variety of reasons, not least that of effectiveness, work with mentally ill people should be a team enterprise. Consequently we hope that this book will be of interest to related professionals such as those entering psychiatry from the medical profession; psychologists; community psychiatric nurses and health visitors.

In Chapter 1 we begin by discussing what is meant by mental illness and then go on to examine some of the conceptual models which have been developed in order to understand it. We extend some space to an explanation of the medical model since it is this view which tends to be the dominant one. However, we indicate that this has come in for challenge in recent years. We then, in Chapter 2, attempt to convey the impact that a mental illness may have upon the individual sufferer, his family, and finally the social worker dealing with the case. We demonstrate that a mental illness can have very wide repercussions, and we discuss the problems of accommodation, employment and finance which it may cause.

In the third chapter the questions of assessment and intervention are introduced. A model for the assessment of mentally ill people and their families is presented, which stresses that the important factors for the social worker are less the specific symptoms of the disorder and more the impacts that these have upon psycho-social functioning. In the second half of this chapter a framework for intervention is described. This explains how the impact of a disorder, upon an individual, may be assigned to one or more of nine modalities. The problems presented in each of these modalities may then be assigned some priority and a focussed intervention attempted. In the past we believe that an unhelpful polarity has developed between the behavioural and the ego-dynamic schools of thought. In this chapter we have attempted to demonstrate how a synthesis of these views and techniques might be achieved.

In Chapter 4 we consider the research evidence for the integrated model discussed in the previous chapter. It is our belief that social work has in the past failed to evaluate adequately the impact of its interventions. This has left it exposed and vulnerable to its critics (Brewer and Lait, 1980). For social work to survive and flourish we believe that it must begin to start marshalling the evidence which demonstrates its value.

In Chapter 5 we cast the net very wide in examining a number of interventive techniques that social workers could easily incorporate into their interventive armoury. In some cases this means looking outside social work to some of the skills developed and utilised by related professions such as psychologists and psychotherapists.

In the next chapter we attempt, by means of a lengthy case study, to demonstrate how a social worker might typically conduct a case. In this instance it concerns a young man suffering from schizophrenia. The case study illustrates the variety of roles that a social worker may be called upon to play, and the variety of interventive techniques he may need to utilise. It also illustrates a number of our other themes, such as the need to co-operate with colleagues.

Most people who suffer from any form of mental illness which brings them into contact with the medical profession will at some time be prescribed drugs. In Chapter 7 we examine the physical treatments used by psychiatrists and family practitioners in their treatment of mental illness, and try to highlight the implications that these may have for the social worker. Whilst social workers are not directly involved in the administration of physical treatments they do have an important role to play, as we make clear.

Social workers are, however, centrally involved in psychiatric emergencies, since they are often the first people called upon to respond. In Chapter 8 we examine the concept of a psychiatric emergency and by reference to the work of Caplan (1964), suggest how something positive may emerge from the situation. In Chapter 9 we concentrate upon one particular type of psychiatric emergency that often causes most anxiety, namely that of suicide. We begin by examining the prevalence of suicide and suicidal behaviour. We then consider how such actions might effectively be predicted and perhaps prevented. Finally, we look at some interventive techniques with those who attempt suicide and with those who may be left bereaved by a successful suicide bid.

In Chapter 10 we review the workings of the Mental Health Act from the social workers' perspective. Particular attention is paid to the 1982 Amendments to the Act which have a number of important implications for social work practice.

The book concludes with a guide to further reading which we hope will prove useful to those readers who might wish to pursue some of the ideas and themes that space has precluded our developing at greater length in the body of this book.

1
What is Meant by Mental Illness

It may seem strange to start a book entitled *Social Work and Mental Illness* by trying to discuss what is meant by mental illness. It is not our intention to seek a definitive definition, nor to replicate what is widely available to standard psychiatric texts. Rather our aim is to suggest that there exist a diversity of views and theories and that the focus for the social worker should always be upon the *consequences* of a particular disorder rather than on its aetiology or detailed pathology. A working knowledge of these aspects of a disorder is obviously an advantage in helping the individual worker to understand his or her clients, appreciate their predicament, discuss issues with colleagues and communicate with others concerned, such as relatives. However, the emphasis must be upon the reality which confronts the client at the time.

It is necessary to preface any further remarks by making a clear distinction between *mental illness* and *mental handicap*. *Mental handicap* implies that an individual is unable to develop beyond certain intellectual limits (the old term was mental deficiency). Usually it results from some form of brain defect or injury which is usually characteristically present from birth, such as Down's Syndrome or Mongolism. In other instances it may be the result of a physical disorder such as hydrocephalus. Treatment in the sense of attempting to produce a 'cure' is impossible in our present state of knowledge. What is required is a supportive environment in which a carefully geared programme of education, tailored to the individual's own pace of learning, help him to maximise his potential. In the past, large hospitals were felt to be the appropriate settings for such efforts. Today the emphasis is upon care in the community or, if that is impossible, the creation of a more home-like atmosphere within the institution.

A *mental illness* on the other hand usually implies that the sufferer has had a period of normality before the illness struck, and that it represents some change in an otherwise normally developing, or developed person. The diagnosis is based upon evidence that an individual is behaving, thinking, or feeling in ways which are unusual or which give him or others cause for concern. The relative importance of disturbances of behaviour, thought or feelings will vary from condition to condition, and hence lead to the application of a different diagnostic label.

The greatest problems tend to hinge on the consideration of what is considered 'unusual'. It is at this point that a degree of relativism has to be introduced and a willingness to look at the wider social context in which the behaviour takes place. As an example let us look at a particular piece of behaviour — hand-washing. In the context of the life of a surgeon, or, one would hope, a butcher, hand-washing forty times a day would not be regarded as unusual. However, in the life of a bank clerk the same pattern would be seen as highly unusual, particularly if it interfered with everyday life and was associated with strong and sometimes frightening fears about dirt and contamination.

This form of relativism, and the need to place behaviour within a wider social context in order to understand it, is thought by many to be unique to the practice of psychiatry. However, it also holds true for many branches of physical medicine. Social, cultural and economic factors all play their part in helping a person decide in the first place that he is ill and in need of attention from a doctor. Medical staff are also influenced by a variety of social factors in forming their diagnosis and deciding upon an appropriate course of action.

The actual forms of behaviour or feelings experienced, may be shared and felt by all of us at some time in our lives. All of us experience changes in mood, for example: days when we feel better than others, when we have plenty of energy and face up to things optimistically. On other occasions we may feel miserable, sluggish and see only the black side of every new situation we meet. Similarly, disturbances of mood of a more profound and long-lasting kind are likely to be experienced during periods of radical change in our lives; starting at a new school, moving house or the loss of somebody who is close to us. Such 'life events' may deeply affect our state of mind, but for most people they are transitory and clearly related to a particular, identifiable aspect of our daily lives, such as loss or change.

Such a disturbance will only begin to be considered a psychiatric disorder when it is either unrelated to an event in our social world, or when the disturbance created by loss or change last longer than would normally be anticipated within the given culture. It is not uncommon to be tearful and depressed on hearing of the death of somebody who is close to one, but it would be treated as a cause for concern if this disturbance persisted for some months and began to interfere seriously with other activities, such as the ability to work.

Many forms of psychiatric disorder are so gross and disabling that this form of cultural relativism does not need to be invoked. However, the fact that ultimately the diagnosis or labelling of somebody as psychiatrically ill, is taken in the absence of any concrete evidence such as can be found in most areas of the physical disorders, has led some people to question the very status of the term 'psychiatric illness'.

The debate which rages within established psychiatric circles, as well as among its many critics is an extremely complicated one which is usefully discussed in two books: *Psychiatry in Dissent* by Anthony Clare and *Reasoning about Madness* by John Wing.

Theorising about mental illness

The dilemma facing those who deal with disturbed people is essentially twofold. First, how may one distinguish between normal and abnormal behaviour? When, for example, does eccentricity, or simply a desire to be different, tip over into something rather more serious? Second, how does one distinguish between reactions of the mind and of the body?

In the attempt to resolve these dilemmas a number of competing theories have emerged. The pre-eminent one, which we may call the medical model, suggests that we treat these disorders as if they were like physical illness. This has many advantages. It means that no blame may be attached to a person who displays the characteristic behaviour or symptoms. It draws people, formerly treated as social pariahs, into the network of conventional medicine. Attempts have been made over the past few years to move away from large institutional settings for the treatment of mental disorders, so that now increasingly the emphasis is placed upon treatment either in the home, or in small specialist units attached to general hospitals. In framing mental disorder in medical terms it may also be that people find the condition more socially acceptable, and are thus more willing to bring forward their difficulties and discuss them. Further support is given to the idea of adopting the medical model for psychiatric disorders by the relative success evidenced by many of the physical treatments now being administered. Advances in the fields of drug therapy and the use of electroconvulsive therapy (ECT) in alleviating much of the distress experienced by those who are psychiatrically disordered, will be detailed later.

This 'medical model' represents the conventionally accepted view of psychiatric disorder. It places the problem squarely in the hands of the medical profession and could be said to have gained general acceptance in a large part of the western world. As a social worker, one has to have a familiarity with the main concepts of this model, and an ability to work within it at least to the extent of gaining the confidence of the medical team. This is particularly important when one is dealing with the more serious forms of disorder. Questioning some of the assumptions of the medical model may be appropriate in the case of individual patients, but outright rejection is likely to lead to a very light case-load and a resultant poor service for the client. We will return to details of the medical model in the next section of this chapter. For a moment we want to look a little more closely at those models which either set out to provide a completely different framework for understanding, or at least challenge in some serious way the conventional wisdom. Many of these are informed by theory which draws from the wider social sciences: sociology, politics, philosophy and psychology. They all tend to shift the focus away from the identified patient and to take a wider view of personal difficulty. In these respects they provide an attractive conceptual framework for the social worker who is essentially unconcerned with any posited basic pathology and rather more with the social implications and impact of resultant behaviours.

The concerns, for many of those who propose alternative models are broadly focused upon three issues:

1. Is it correct to ascribe the word *illness* to psychiatric disorder?
2. Are doctors in danger of applying the label of psychiatric illness to problems of daily living? Replicating the kind of medical colonisation that has taken place with problems such as alcoholism, and has been attempted with delinquency and criminal behaviour?
3. Is psychiatric intervention destructive – either physically by way of the treatments it offers or socially by the application of a stigmatising label?

One of the leading critics, the American Thomas Szasz, who is an advocate of a new model, is himself a psychiatrist although practising as an analyst. In 1960 he wrote a short paper entitled 'The myth of mental illness' which was subsequently expanded into a book of the same name. Although he has gone on to write at length on this theme the original paper contains the seed for all his subsequent works. In it he argued that the term 'illness', when attributed to mental disorder, was really only being used as a metaphor. Doctors treated people who acted strangely *as if* they were ill. Subsequently as the discipline of psychiatry developed, the *'as if'* began to be dropped, and people were treated *as ill*. The 'myth of mental illness' was thus created. What people are really suffering from, he argues, are not diseases, but 'problems of living'. He bases this view upon the fact that no physical lesion or malfunctioning of a causal kind is identifiable in those deemed to be suffering from a mental illness. He goes on to make the point that should any physical pathology ever be discovered the relevant syndrome would be immediately redefined as a physical illness and shifted into another medical specialism such as neurology. He mentions as an example the case of mental disturbances resulting from syphilitic infection. Before the detection and isolation of the infective matter this form of disturbance was treated as a type of psychiatric disorder rather than the physical illness we regard it as today. However, in adopting this line of logical argument Szasz fails to document those many cases of purely physical disorder which remain impossible to detect and diagnose by some physical test or demonstration of a lesion. The fact that we cannot produce that form of physical evidence has not stopped doctors in the past — nor indeed the present — proceeding to treat such patients with whatever seemed to be effective in bringing about a cure or a relief of the symptoms.

In tone, his criticisms of conventional psychiatry share something of those mounted by the British psychiatrist R. D. Laing (1970, 1971). However, the underlying attitudes of the two men are sharply at odds. Szasz is inbred with the notions of free market capitalism, wherein the only legitimate contract is that freely struck between doctors and patient. Laing approaches the dilemma from the direction of the libertarian left. His ideas have been developed over a diverse series of books, and it is not always possible to see any consistent links. He would appear to have shifted ground on a number of occasions whilst seeming to retain the same basic hostility to the conventional medical view of psychiatric disorder. He draws some support for his ideas from existential philosophers such as Jean-Paul Sartre (1969), with their conviction that all forms of human behaviour have validity. This leads him to the belief that psychotic behaviour, previously considered by many to be bizarre and irrational, in fact has meaning and should be appreciated and valued, rather than simply seen as the manifestation of disordered thinking. This identification with the psychotic patient has led him to talk of the illness in terms of a 'journey' into madness, a voyage to a different level of experience. At some points in his work he lays emphasis upon the idea, familiar to family therapists, that 'the patient' is really only responding to the crazy world around him. In his view the patient is being pushed into madness in order to escape the otherwise inescapable tensions and paradoxes of everyday life. At this point his thinking moves him closest to those mainly American theorists who see psychiatric disorder as understandable in terms of faulty communication patterns between the 'patient' and the wider world. Workers such as Bateson (1956), Wynne (1958) and Lidz (1965), have suggested that in order fully to understand the nature of psychiatric disorder we must examine the intimate network of social relationships, usually familial, in which the 'patient' operates. Both Szasz and Laing still manage, despite their reservations, to work as psychiatrists and to help people in distress.

Another powerful critique has come from those outside the professional arena who approach the study of psychiatric disorder, and its institutions from the field of sociology. Erving Goffman (1961), author of the important and eminently readable account of life inside an American psychiatric hospital, *Asylums*, suggests that patients suffer not from an illness, but a set of life-circumstances or adverse contingencies. Patients would avoid the tag of illness if they were able to be supported by a network of relatives, good housing and a stable job. The importance of this perspective will not be lost on anybody who has worked in a large hospital for chronic psychiatric patients. Many certainly appear to be confined because of the lack of any appropriate alternative place to live rather than because of their symptomatology. Many appear to be not so much ill as failing to cope with the rigours and demands of a world which expects regular attendance at work, and a conventional repertoire of social responses and relationships. The inroads made by schemes such as group-homes and day-centres offering employment, indicate that to a limited extent at least, Goffman may be correct in his assessment.

Thomas Scheff (1966), has tried to draw upon labelling theory more frequently linked with deviancy such as criminal behaviour, in order to advance his argument. In his view mental illness is essentially a form of rule-breaking, and what is of primary importance is not the original violation of social norms but rather the reaction of the audience to it. He suggests that we develop, via the popular imagery of television and newspapers, a stereotyped idea of somebody who is 'nuts' or 'looney'.

When the rule breaker is viewed in these terms a whole series of social ramifications result in the formation of what is termed 'secondary deviance'. These residual rule-breakers, who don't fit into any other obvious category such as criminal, are then ascribed the label of mental illness. The label carries with it an expectation that the individual will adopt a certain role and perform in a stereotyped way. Within this model the disordered behaviour and subsequent label of mental illness has less to do with individual pathology and rather more to do with the audience's reaction to the initial rule-breaking.

Scheff fails to explain the original violation of the norms, as he freely admits. What he is able to do is to draw attention, via his theory, to those powerful secondary effects which may be attendant upon our labelling somebody as psychiatrically ill. The repercussions of such labelling may be profound and serve to reinforce and maintain the individual in the position in which he finds himself. The repercussions of labelling somebody are beginning to be appreciated by medical staff. This may be observed in the cautious ways in which labels are applied to the young. The reluctance to describe a teenager as schizophrenic results in the use of terms such as 'schizophrenic behaviour' at case conferences and referral letters. The 'stickiness' of a psychiatric label is such that it may have to be carried for the rest of the person's life.

The power of such labels will not be disputed by those who have tried to obtain employment for an ex-psychiatric patient. The difficulties that younger people in particular have, in explaining a hospitalisation to work — or school — colleagues, and the subsequent mockery and rejection they may have to suffer, are yet other examples of the power of labels.

Hans Eysenck, a British psychologist, is more limited in the attacks he makes. He sees the whole field of psychiatry as being much too wide and whilst acknowledging the role of medicine in the more severe psychotic disorders, argues for the primacy of psychology in the understanding and treatment of what are generally regarded as the neuroses (Eysenck, 1975). He bases this stand upon the assumption that various forms of behavioural treatment, which concentrate upon the modification of overt behaviours, are markedly superior to the conventional medical ones when applied to neurotics. For him, rather like Szasz, neurotic illness is not pathology based upon a physical lesion, but rather the inability to adapt and cope with everyday life. What is required is not medication but a form of intensive social education.

The danger in adopting any of these theories in a wholesale way is that when fully explicated they tend to be as full of logical holes as does the strictly medical model. The inconsistencies in some of the alternative theories are well examined by Peter Sedgwick in his book *Psycho-Politics* (1982).

Siegler and Osmond (1966) have attempted, at least for psychotic illness, to spell out what each of a series of models implies in terms of interventive strategies. They present what they call the following models of madness — medical, moral, impaired, psychoanalytical, social, psychedelic, conspiratorial and familial. Some of these models remain sketchy in their presentation but the attempt to think through the implications of each one is thought-provoking.

Medical models of mental illness

The critics of conventional psychiatry, have, in their various ways, pointed to some of the deficiencies and inconsistencies in current practice. That these difficulties exist would be denied by few psychiatrists who actually think deeply about the many professional tasks that they are called upon to undertake. However, most would argue that they are presented daily, sometimes in overwhelming numbers, with people in distress, whether as patients or their families. The model of understanding and intervention that they have developed is essentially pragmatic and as such, in the hands of good practitioners, flexible enough to accommodate a number of different models. These models may be framed within a fairly conventional system of classification of the symptoms observed, but are wide enough to encompass medical, social, psychological and rehabilitative modes of intervention.

A good psychiatrist should be able to undertake a full medical investigation of the patient, gather a rounded understanding of his or her social position, including information about housing, employment and social relationships. Too often the critics of psychiatry are, quite reasonably, criticising poor practice rather than the principles which lie behind it. A competent psychiatrist should be able to make use, where appropriate, of drugs and other physical treatments; basic counselling skills, environmental manipulation such as assistance and advice about employment and finding somewhere to live; as well as be able to discuss the patient's problems with his or her family, if any, and help in the rehabilitation and reintegration which may be necessary.

A simple, but by no means clear-cut distinction is usually made between those mental disorders deemed neurotic and those psychotic. John Wing (1978) offers the following definition.

A 'psychotic' state is one characterised by delusions or hallucinations, in which the individual is unable to differentiate his grossly abnormal thought processes from external reality and remains unaware of his deficiency. A 'neurotic' state is one in which the psychological abnormalities are much less severe, in the sense that they do not interfere with the discrimination between internal and external worlds and the individual is well aware that he has obsessions or phobias, though the knowledge may not help him to understand them.

However, useful as this distinction is, Wing points out that because of fluctuations within a condition, it is quite possible for somebody with a psychotic disorder to be quite lucid and insightful, whilst somebody in a severe neurotic state may act in blind panic, and be quite unable to control their own behaviour.

In attempting now to offer a simplified classification of psychiatric disorders, we risk giving the impression of order and consistency, when in fact reality is far more complex.

Any diagnosis, in psychiatry, is likely to be coloured by the individual's previous personality and by the particular events surrounding the current disturbance. It is not uncommon, as with physical illness, for the symptoms to flare and subside so that some diagnoses that are offered may be provisional and subject to change. For heuristic purposes we intend to describe the various syndromes under these five headings: organic psychoses; functional psychoses; affective disorders; neuroses; personality disorders.

Organic psychoses

The organic mental states are traditionally sub-divided into acute and chronic conditions. All are created by some disturbance to the workings of the brain, and hence have been described as 'bodily based psychoses'. As a rule of thumb the acute (or 'reversible') states are characterised by clouding of consciousness, while the chronic (or 'irreversible') states are accompanied by a deterioration in personality and intelligence.

The acute conditions may be produced in five ways:

(a)   metabolic disturbance
(b)   the toxic effect of drugs
(c)   rapid withdrawal of drugs including alcohol
(d)   infections
(e)   trauma to the brain.

The results, in most cases, are a combination of the following six symptoms:

(a)   clouding of consciousness − the individual appears drowsy and not fully alert
(b)   disorientation: unable to locate himself in time and place, attention is affected and distraction level is high
(c)   memory; impaired memory during period of confusion
(d)   perception; may misinterpret things − illusions
(e)   speech and thought: typically fragmented and disconnected
(f)   mood: variations of mood including feelings of fear.

The individual is unlikely to be co-operative since his ability to comprehend is limited. Social work intervention should be restricted to rapidly alerting the medical services and continuing to work with the anxieties of any relatives. Many of these disorders respond quickly once the underlying medical causation is discovered. This may involve the treatment of an infective disorder or making good some metabolic disturbance by means of vitamins.

The chronic disorders are most usually some form of dementia – the destruction of some part of the brain. This is a process shared by all of us as we age. However, in some people the process starts rather earlier than normal or advances more rapidly. The symptomatology asserts itself in four areas:

1. *Impairment of memory:* initially this is confined to recent events but as the disease progresses earlier events are affected. In the early stages the individual may be aware of the process and be able to push back its effects by keeping notes and self-reminders
2. *Deterioration in intellect:* problem-solving capacity is reduced, particularly with regard to abstract calculations
3. *Emotional:* increased lability; crying and laughing for little apparent reason
4. *Behaviour:* gradually personal habits deteriorate so that the house and clothing become neglected.

Treatment is such cases may be very limited and restricted to attempts to ensure a good diet and vitamin sufficiency. An important issue for the social worker may be the patient's need for institutionalisation. Most of the care may well rest on the family and any support that they can be given – be it financial, moral or physical – will contribute to the length of time the individual can resist the need for institutional care. Increasing efforts are being made to develop alternatives to this either/or situation. The use of beds for short fixed periods of time (rotating or holiday relief beds) as a respite in order to provide assistance and relief to relatives is being promoted. Similarly, the use of sheltered housing, visiting wardens and home-helps may contribute to somebody's remaining in the community.

Functional psychoses

This group of disorders receives the name functional from the fact that usually no structural or organic cause has yet been discovered to account for them. Diagnosis relies upon identifying an impairment of normal mental functioning.

The major disorder contained under this heading is *schizophrenia*. It is perhaps more accurate to talk of the schizophrenias, because whilst at present the disorder is conventionally sub-divided into four different types, it seems likely that as we discover ever more about it further subdivisions will be discovered. Although people suffering from this disorder do share enough common characteristics for them to be grouped together, each person tends to be unique in his or her presentation of the finer-grained symptoms. Any number of definitions have been advanced in order to try to encapsulate the disorder. Perhaps the most widely used, at least in Britain, is that which relies upon Kurt Schneider's listing of 'first rank symptoms' (1959). The presence of any one of these, in the absence of evidence of epilepsy, intoxication (by drink or drugs) and gross brain damage is taken as sound indication of the presence of the disorder. The symptoms he describes are as follows:

(a) hearing one's own thoughts spoken aloud in one's own head
(b) the experience that one's thoughts are repeated after one has thought them
(c) the experience of alien thoughts being planted into one's own mind
(d) experiencing one's own will being replaced or taken over by some outside force
(e) experiencing that several voices are commenting, between themselves, upon one's own thoughts or actions.

These may be summarised in the following three ways:

(a) feelings of passivity
(b) auditory hallucinations in the third person
(c) primary delusions.

Feelings of passivity, may be said to exist, when the individual has the experience that his thoughts, feelings and actions are not his own, and that he is made to do things by outside influences. Typically, these days, such feelings are attributed to 'rays' or forces emanating from the television.

At this point it might prove helpful if we distinguish between three terms which are commonly used in psychiatry — illusion, hallucination and delusion. An *illusion* is the misinterpretation of a real stimulus. Examples might be seeing a flapping curtain as a bat or hearing a distant stream as a group of people muttering. An *hallucination*, on the other hand, is a perception which has no such objective basis. Any of the senses may be affected. Typically a person may hear voices, or feel things crawling on his flesh. A *delusion* is a false belief, which is nonetheless firmly held. For example, somebody may believe that he is the cause of an air-crash, or responsible for all the evil in the world.

Schizophrenia is a fairly common disorder affecting approximately 1 per cent of the population. About three-quarters of the cases are detected in people between the ages of 17 and 25. The origins of this puzzling condition are still unclear, with sometimes heated arguments breaking out among those who advance biochemical, genetic, or socio/-psychological theories. In the case of identical (*monozygotic*) twins, it has been estimated that if one twin is diagnosed as suffering from the disorder, then the chance that the other will be similarly diagnosed lies between 35 and 65 per cent. This is referred to as a *concordance rate*. In instances where both parents have been diagnosed as schizophrenic, there is a 41 per cent chance that their children will be similarly affected. If one parent is schizophrenic then 12 per cent of the offspring will be too, while 33 per cent will have schizoid personalities. Such figures still leave open the possibility that environment and early socialisation play a part in what could be a multi-factoral cause.

The schizophrenias are divided into the following four broad types, each characterised by the pattern of onset and certain other characteristic features:
(a) *simple schizophrenia*
(b) *hebephrenic schizophrenia*
(c) *catatonic schizophrenia*
(d) *paranoid schizophrenia.*

Simple schizophrenia is usually described as having an insidious onset, with a gradual social deterioration being experienced over a period of time. Typically individuals appear rather withdrawn, lack interest in things around them, are apathetic, have difficulty in making and maintaining social contacts, and begin to display a drop-off in performance, particularly intellectual. It is easy to see how this type of behaviour, exhibited in an adolescent, may be mistaken for boredom with school, drug taking, or difficulty in adjusting to an adult role. In people a little older work-performance is affected, and job loss may follow. A typical picture is then one of a downward drift through the social strata, lowered income, and poor housing contributing to the downward spiral. Many schizophrenics of this type end their days in prison, cheap rooming-houses or hostels, living a nomadic, tramp-like existence, often complicated by a drinking problem.

Hebephrenia may also present with an insidious onset, but is characterised by emotional abnormality and thought-disorder. Thinking may be affected in a number of ways. Most commonly the individual finds difficulty in thinking in abstract terms. This may give a strangeness to responses during conversation since the concrete aspects of any subject are stressed. Thinking may also be over-inclusive, with many irrelevancies. Thought-blocking may also occur; here the individual simply stops the flow of the conversation and may resume on a different subject area. All of this may make any attempt at an interview bewildering and perplexing. If the social worker is not prepared for this strangeness he or she may find that it makes them feel uncomfortable. It may prove necessary to work more slowly, emphasise very simple points, use repetition, and if necessary, return on another occasion. Typically the expression of emotion is inappropriate, with a good deal of seemingly unprovoked smiling and giggling. Frequently the individual is subject to auditory hallucinations, and may indulge in rather silly, or even mischievous behaviour, as well as exhibiting facial grimacing and an oddity of manner.

The third type of schizophrenia is referred to as *catatonia*. This has a sudden onset and may create in the individual a state varying from stupor to acute excitement. It is most commonly typified as resulting in the patient sitting or standing rather rigidly in a fixed position. In practice this form of the illness is now quite rarely seen, perhaps because of the various anti-psychotic drugs now so widely used. What may still be noticed more frequently are some of the following:-

Negativism — the expression of behaviour that is the opposite of what would be normal or expected response.
Echolalia and *echopraxia* — the involuntary and meaningless repetition of words and actions.
Automatic obedience.

Finally, and usually starting somewhat later in life than the other forms, is *paranoid schizophrenia.* This is typified by hallucinations and delusions of persecution. The individual's personality may remain remarkably unimpaired, so that in normal conversation he may appear reasonably lucid and rational. However, if the seat of the delusion is mentioned in conversation the person may become rather agitated and emotional. In some cases the delusion is explained with a good deal of pseudo-logic so that it is not uncommon, at least initially, to be taken in by an account and believe it to be true. A case comes to mind of a man in his mid seventies who described a supposedly thwarted love affair with a woman from across the street, which had resulted in his twice knocking her to the ground, after accusing her of going with other men whom she had met as a nightclub hostess. The woman in question turned out to be in her eighties and only left her home once a week to visit her daughter.

Affective disorders

Depression and mania are disorders in which the primary symptom is one of mood-change. The incidence of such disorders, which demand treatment, is 3–4 per 1,000 of the population. However, milder forms of depression, described in the next section as neuroses, are extremely common. Estimates suggest that between 13 and 15 per cent of the general population suffer a milder form of depression at some time during their lives.

Many classificatory systems exist for these disorders. Terms such as reactive and endogenous, psychological and physical, retarded and agitated, are sometimes used by adherents of competing schools of thought. The relationship between depression and mania is also the subject of some controversy. Some people appear to suffer extreme mood-swings (*cyclothymia*) which produce alternating periods of mania and depression. Others seem to have simply a pattern of periodic depression. The genetic evidence is also cloudy but would appear to support the view that heredity is an important factor, particularly in the case of manic-depressive disorders.

Mania

Mania is typified by a mood-state of elation and excitement. In its milder form, *hypomania*, it may be necessary to have some knowledge of the person's previous personality in order to make a distinction between his present state and his normal behaviour. Typically sufferers appear to be driven along by some internal force, such that speech, thoughts and action are speeded up. In conversation they are often difficult to follow since the words flow at a great rate and, because they are highly distractable, the subject may change rapidly. They may indulge in vigorous bouts of physical activity, stopping, however, before the chosen task is completed. During an interview their mood of elation may be catching and it is easy to be drawn into their enthusiasms by the warmth they display. Meeting such people for the first time one might be tempted to ask 'what's the problem?', so obviously are they enjoying life. However, the mood-state, if it persists, rapidly uses up the patience of people close to the sufferers who, in turn, may get into all kinds of scrapes. They may be extremely liberal with their money, ordering expensive cars or demanding to drive around in a taxi for hours. The strains imposed upon their families by this sort of larger-than-life behaviour are obvious. They may also indulge in other activities to excess, heavy drinking and sexual activity, for example.

In severe cases the mania may become so powerful that the individual, by his ceaseless activity and refusal to eat, may present a danger to himself. Eventually in such cases a state of exhaustion is reached, often shared by those around the individual.

Mania is one of the instances when the social worker may be under some pressure to admit the individual to hospital under a compulsory order (see Chapter 10). His lifestyle may be causing severe difficulties for other people, and he may be endangering himself — one of our clients insisted upon trying to stop the traffic on a busy main road with his head, for example.

Social work intervention may have to be restricted to support for relatives and in trying to extricate the individual from some of the social consequences of his actions. In the case of one woman client this involved returning a number of mink coats to various furriers and trying to obtain refunds for a desperate family faced with mounting bills. Direct work with a client is dependent upon the degree of the mania. It may well be a waste of effort since little information is likely to be retained. Effective contact may have to wait until either the medication takes effect or the disorder runs its course.

Neuroses

The neuroses may perhaps best be viewed as reactions of particular personality types to stress, real or imagined. A classification, again highly simplified, like the following is commonly presented:

(a) anxiety states
(b) phobias
(c) obsessional states
(d) depression
(e) hysteria.

Many of these may present themselves as either exaggerations, or extensions of normal behaviour, and as such are commonly experienced by all of us at some time in our lives. This makes them more comprehensible to the layman, but at the same time may lead people to suggest to those afflicted that all they need to do is to pull themselves together, or 'get on and do something to take your mind off it'. Although similar to everyday experience they are seen as illness because they are long-lasting, interfere with normal life and are ultimately life-threatening.

An *anxiety state* is a good example of this, since we all of us at some time are confronted by situations which arouse in us strong feelings of anxiety. The clinical state is characterised by prolonged and excessive feelings of anxiety, seemingly unrelated to any realistic external stimuli. The subjective feeling is often accompanied by physiological changes of various kinds. These may include the following:

(a)   sweating
(b)   palpitations
(c)   nausea
(d)   raised blood pressure
(e)   gastric upsets
(f)   frequency of micturition
(g)   dryness of the mouth.

At times the level of anxiety may become so acute that it results in a panic attack. Here the person may scream and shout in terror, appear uncontrolled and extremely disorganised. In such a state self-harm, or accidental injury, is a danger.

If the anxiety is focused upon some particular object or class of objects it is usually described as a *phobia*. The symptoms experienced, and behaviour evidenced, are similar to those described above. However, they usually subside in the absence of the anxiety-producing object. Two of the commonest are *agoraphobia* − a dread of open spaces − and *claustrophobia* − the fear of enclosed spaces. Other common ones are associated with cats, snakes, and flying. In some cases the problem can be contained by the individual simply by avoiding the phobic situation or object. For example, a fear of snakes or flying may not pose a problem if one lives in a city, and has no need to travel long distances. However, in other instances the phobia may gradually restrict the person's life-style and social contacts, so that his life becomes isolated and impoverished.

The *obsessive-compulsive* states may also be seen as an exaggeration of normal behaviours, since many of us perform small, repetitive routines in our daily lives — checking that our wallet is in our pocket or purse in bag, for example. For those to be seen as a clinical problem they must be seen to be disrupting normal patterns of life. A bank clerk who routinely checks and rechecks money before handing it across the counter may be simply conscientious; when he becomes unable ever to release the money to the customer, as happened to one of our clients, then it begins to be a problem not only for him but also for his employer.

Obsessions are essentially fixed or repetitive thought-patterns or ideas in the individual's mind, whilst compulsions are acts which the individual feels compelled to carry out. Both forms of behaviour may be observable in other psychiatric syndromes, for example somebody suffering from schizophrenia or depression may share some of this symptomatology. However, in these cases other more serious symptoms are also fairly obvious. Common patterns among individuals affected do emerge; for example, endless checking of door-locks, or gas-taps is quite common as is handwashing and repetitive touching of objects.

The term *depression* covers a wide spectrum of disorder as we saw in the earlier section on affective disorders. At one extreme it may be used (as earlier) to describe a condition so severe that the individual is quite out of touch with reality, grossly retarded, and displaying some of the symptoms associated with psychoses. At the other it may be used to describe a milder upset of mood closely related to some external life event such as bereavement or loss of a job. For many of these people it will be transitory and self-limiting, for others it will involve lengthy periods of hospitalisation and the increased risk of suicide.

The symptomatology may be split into two — the psychological and the physical. Psychologically the individual will be miserable, gloomy in conversation and display a loss of vitality and interest. He or she may appear rather withdrawn with a slowing of speech and movement. Concentration tends to suffer, and he or she may express feelings of guilt. In some cases the melancholy will centre on a concern for his or her physical health, with many hypochondrical complaints being made. Physically the depressed person is likely to complain of difficulties in sleeping or eating (with consequent weight loss) and loss of libido.

Hysteria, at least in its more extreme forms, is now fairly rare in adults, although still seen among children. It consists of a shifting of emotional conflict, be it fear or anxiety, from mental symptoms onto physical ones. In doing so the individual may incapacitate him- or herself, but is afforded some so-called 'secondary gains'. These occur because the apparent physical disability or paralysis may result in the person receiving a good deal of extra attention, whilst having lessened demands made upon them. All of this is a motivation which remains unrecognised by the patient. The actual behaviour displayed may vary widely. A limb may appear to be extremely weak or totally paralysed; the person may display tics and tremors; he or she may claim a loss of one of the senses — hysterical blindness, for example, and in some cases appear unable to speak.

Personality disorders

Finally, we come to what is something of a psychiatric rag-bag: namely personality disorders. The simplest definition depicts them as resulting from an abnormal personality and some environmental stressor. However, it is something of a grey area, and many people, psychiatrists among them, have argued that general psychiatry has little part to play in such problems, and that doctors and others have been guilty of a kind of colonialism, carving out for themselves new areas of professional expertise. Many doctors would agree with the view that the help they are able to give is limited. However, the fact is that daily they are presented with such people who ask for help in a variety of ways to relieve the distress that they experience. The problems which they present are essentially those in which the individual has a difficulty in adapting to the particular society in which they find themselves, and problems in adjusting to prevailing social norms. The societal dimension is extremely important since, under a different set of circumstances, it is possible to imagine the individual coping quite adequately in many cases. Many of the labels applied — depressive personality, obsessive personality, schizoid personality, and so on — are really only watered-down examples of the traits we have already described. It is doubtful how much conventional psychiatric medicine, if that can be taken to mean the usual range of drugs and physical treatments, has to offer. Usually what are required are counselling, environmental manipulation, and psychological techniques such as training in social skills. Attempting to change somebody's personality is clearly an awesome task. What may be more successful is either modifying the environment in which he or she operates or teaching him or her a new set of skills or behaviours so that he or she may interact more smoothly and effectively with the world around.

Conclusion

We have tried to convey something of the flavour of the debate about current psychiatric practice and the standard classificatory system adopted by psychiatrists. Any social worker dealing with those deemed mentally ill should familiarise themselves with the standard psychiatric texts, some of which are referred to in the list of further reading, so that they may appreciate the concepts with which colleagues are likely to be working. This should not be taken to imply that social workers should simply take on board the entire medical model of mental illness. The concerns of the social worker are essentially different from those of the psychiatrist and this should be reflected in the way in which the individual is viewed. The social worker is less concerned about diagnostic nicety, and possible underlying pathology. Their focus should be upon present funtioning and adjustment to surroundings. The approach the social worker adopts is closer to a rehabilitative model than a medical one. He or she should be concerned to discover the clients' current strengths and help them to develop strategies whereby they can make the most of their current life situation.

2

The Impact of Mental Disorder

In our first chapter we have examined briefly the traditional model of mental illness and reviewed some of the challenges to it. We indicated that whilst the social worker might find some of the alternatives that we described attractive, in order to communicate with colleagues such as psychiatrists, nurses and psychologists, familiarity with the language and concepts of the medical model is necessary. However, the social worker's focus is essentially different from that of colleagues and it is specifically the social work view of problems that we wish to examine in this chapter and the next. For the social worker the niceties of diagnosis are less important than the client's present functioning and the impact that has upon the individual, the individual's family and their wider social circle.

The type of disorder from which the client may be suffering is, from a social worker's perspective, of less relevance than its wider ramifications. In order to assess the situation fully and offer an appropriate intervention the social worker should have in mind four important guiding principles:

(a) the *uniqueness of the manifestation*
(b) the difference between the *form* and the *content* of the disorder
(c) the *meaning* attributed to the disorder by the individual and significant others
(d) attempts made by the individual and significant others to *normalise* the effects of the disorder.

Unique manifestation

The first of these four points was neatly summed up by Max Hamilton, formerly Professor of Psychiatry at the University of Leeds in a personal communication. He said 'No matter how classic the symptoms are, the experience of the illness is demonstrated via the individual's own personality and their particular social circumstances; consequently, every time we see a mentally ill person we are observing a *unique manifestation* of the syndrome'. The emphasis upon the uniqueness of the individual is an important antidote to the tendency, within the medical world, to treat people who are given the same psychiatric label as if they shared many other characteristics. It is one of the social worker's tasks to individualise the client and try to place his or her problems within some wider framework of understanding, whilst attempting to tease out the specific implications that a particular clinical manifestation might have for that individual and see it within the context of an earlier and ongoing social world.

Form and content

The second general point to consider is that the social worker should be able to appreciate the differences between the form and the content of the disorder. For the psychiatrist the form of the disorder — the distinctive patterning of behaviour and feelings — may be of paramount importance for it leads to a diagnosis. However, for the social worker, greater attention should paid to the content, for it is by this means that some understanding of the nature of the disorder from the client's perspective may be appreciated. The form of presentation might lead to a diagnosis of depression, for which the pyschiatrist prescribes certain drugs. The content of the client's talk may indicate to the social worker where a start is to be made in unravelling the particular set of difficulties with which the client arrives and the particular order of priorities the client attaches to them. The content of the conversation will also indicate if specific social or familiar pressures, external to the individual, are creating or exacerbating the disorder.

The meaning of disorder

The third element to consider is the particular meaning that the disorder might have for the client and for those around him. The disorder may be perceived in a distorted way because of some psychotic process, but it is nonetheless important to grasp how the individual concerned, and those significant others in his life, make sense of what is going on. At its simplest we usually attempt to explain some upset or disorder in our lives by reference to something that has happened in the past. An example would be that of a mother offering a fall down the cellar steps in infancy as an explanation for her adolescent's current bizarre behaviour. This explanation may be offered out of a sense of guilt or simply as the only way in which the individual can come to terms with the disturbing events now occurring. These lay explanations for the disorder are important because they may colour the information that is given about the problem and affect things such as the willingness to accept and comply with treatment as well as any desire or encouragement to get better.

Attempts at normalisation

The final common factor to consider is that frequently a client will attempt to control and suppress his or her difficulties in an attempt to appear as normal as possible. This may mean that feelings and ideas are hidden from others for fear that they will frighten or disturb. Those around the client may detect a desire to be alone or a general closing-down of emotional and communication channels. The bewilderment felt by the individual may also be denied as he tries to retain a sense of internal balance against the strong forces attempting to overwhelm him. The strain of attempting to retain control of strongly felt emotions and ideations can be extremely taxing and may make them seem tense, irritable and strained to those around them. The social worker has the task of gaining the clients' confidence and empathising with the uniqueness of their struggles to retain rationality and control alarming emotions. Almost regardless of what clinical label is applied to the individual, the social worker should be mindful of these four factors as they begin the task of creating a therapeutic contract.

The impact of mental illness upon the individual

In order to understand the impact of mental illness upon an individual and that individual's family, we will have to compartmentalise artificially a process which is in reality a tightly interlocked system which is both *intra*-active (occurring within the person) and *inter*-active (occurring between people). In order to begin we have chosen to start by examining the impact upon the individual client.

At the start of the psychiatric breakdown the client may sense a vague feeling of unease, with perhaps uncontrollable ideas breaking into his conscious thoughts. This may create a sense of confusion within the individual's mind and begin to disrupt normal, logical thinking. The individual generally struggles against these imposed ideas and attempts to retain a sense of equilibrium. For a period this may be successful and the individual feels his or her usual self. However, these feelings will engender distress as they undermine the individual's understanding of day-to-day experiences. The failure to understand and control one's own feelings and thoughts is alarming. One young man suffering from his first schizophrenic episode recalled to one of us that he was horrified to find 'thoughts in my head that weren't mine'; whilst a woman suffering from depression said 'I know I've nothing to be depressed about, but I can't stop my feelings'. Within our culture we expect people to retain control of their emotions and feelings except under exceptional circumstances such as sudden bereavement, so the fear of losing control and displaying strong emotion, such as tearfulness or intense misery, is extremely worrying.

In the case of a psychotic experience the very bizarreness of the hallucination may add an extra dimension to the fear that the person is losing control of part of his life. One of the earliest generalised feelings is probably that of *incomprehension*. The client does not appear to understand what is going wrong, knowing only that once-familiar ideas, moods, feelings and physical responses are being interrupted and distorted. The feeling of bewilderment engendered may lead to a state of *anxiety* and *uncertainty*. There then may follow a *distortion of communication* as the client finds difficulty in expressing himself and in turn in comprehending what others are saying. The disruption of normal communication may itself then lead to further misunderstandings and difficulties between the client, his family and others and so a vicious spiral develops.

At this point the individual may begin to question his own state and begin to express fears about 'going mad'. Within every culture sterotypes of mad behaviour are learned (Scheff, 1966), and it is these ideas which begin to figure prominently in the client's thinking. Learned ideas about what mad people do, how they are viewed and treated by others, and where they might end, begin to trouble the client. To accompany this may come a feeling of *rejection* and emotional isolation. The client in seeking to minimise the emotional demands that people make, may shun others. In turn this may provoke a reaction from family and friends who may then further reinforce these initial feelings of rejection. This again may lead to feelings of *aggression* as the client becomes angry with himself and others. This in turn may alienate people further and may well be the emotional state which greets the social workers on first contact with client and family. Finally, as the difficulties in coping with everyday life increase, a feeling of *inadequacy* overtakes the individual, leading him to feel hopeless and depressed.

What we have attempted to convey is the way in which somebody entering upon a psychiatric illness passes through a series of emotional states, some of which are engendered or reinforced by the attitudes and behaviour of others. These emotional states may not be directly caused by the psychiatric disorder, but they do result from it. Graphically this might be depicted (Figure 2.1) as a kind of vortex of self-reinforcing emotions, into which the individual is sucked.

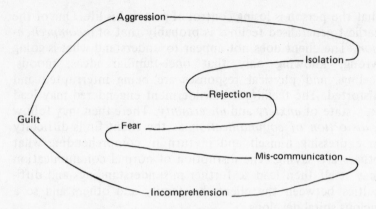

Figure 2.1 *The vortex of psychiatric experience*

Impact upon the family

The individual's self-identity is maintained by the responses of other people. In everyday life we all perform a number of different roles, husband, brother, worker, etc., in relation to those significant other people in our lives. As a mental illness progresses some of these roles may be disrupted, as the individual finds it harder to meet his responsibilities and the expectations of others. The uncertainty and unpredictability engendered in social relationships may erode the tolerance of the family and this can be an important factor in the request for hospital admission, as Greenley (1979) among others demonstrates.

The impact that a mental disorder may have upon an individual's family and significant others in their life is therefore an important dimension to the problem, and one in which a social worker must often involve himself. Frequently on first contact the family may appear *hostile* and *defensive* and it may be too easy in such circumstances to attribute a degree of blame to them for the disorder. However, a more sympathetic reading of the situation is usually possible. Relatives may have had to endure a good deal of difficult behaviour from the client so that what meets the social worker on a first visit may be a good deal of pent up feeling of frustration and anger, tinged with a little guilt. Part of the social work task is to disentangle these feelings, help the individuals concerned to some appreciation of how they have arisen and attempt to enable them to come to some resolution.

The interpretation of these emotions to other professionals may also be a task for the social worker. Staff working with the client in an institutional setting, such as a hospital, may project onto the family all kinds of negative feelings that have grown because of their partial view of the circumstances. We can well remember the negative attitude and open hostility expressed by ward-staff to the parents of a young autistic child admitted to hospital. The staff quickly gained the impression that the parents were emotionally cold towards the child and overtly rejecting. However, after some weeks on the ward, nursing staff had begun to appreciate how the child's own flattened emotional responses might engender such feelings within the parents. Meanwhile, time spent by the social worker with the parents revealed that they were deeply attached to the child, but bewildered by its responses and defending themselves against the pain that this caused.

In such cases the social worker's role of go-between and interpreter may help to soften entrenched attitudes and stereotyped views.

The family response to psychiatric illness

A number of common responses typically adopted by the family may be noted. First, there is usually a feeling of incomprehension which the social worker can do something to allay by explaining the nature of the illness, a likely prognosis and possible treatments. Second, the early stages of the illness may have exaggerated existing disharmony within the family. Somehow the distortions of communication and the strain of coping with somebody becoming ill opens up cracks in many families and reactivates long-buried disagreements. Inevitably some members of the family will feel guilty about what has happened either because of things they have said or done in the past, or left unsaid and undone. Some may also be rather fearful of mental illness and the image that psychiatric hospitals and treatments conjure up. The fear could also be associated with doubts that they may harbour about their own state of health or mind. Mental illness still constitutes a stigma to many people and the family may have to bear the brunt of this. This may lead them to conceal the facts from friends and neighbours thereby further isolating themselves and the patient.

The recognition of client and family need

The needs of the client and his family may be assigned to one of three broad categories:

(a) emotional
(b) socio-economic
(c) physical.

It is important that the social worker be aware of these three dimensions since, because they are all inter-related, an intervention might be required in any one or indeed all of them. So far in this discussion we have concentrated upon the dimension of emotion. However, socio-economic need is a major field for social work intervention and it is this that we intend to discuss next. With regard to physical need, which we examine in the subsequent section, the social work role is less that of a direct intervention and more of a monitoring one.

Socio-economic needs

Freud noted that 'work binds the individual to reality' and certainly the need for employment, or its maintenance, may be of high priority. In the 1980s this is, however, becoming more difficult to achieve as unemployment increases and employers have a larger pool of potential labour to call upon. Many studies, including that of Wansbrough and Cooper (1980) have indicated the importance of employment to the rehabilitation and resettlement of those who have suffered from a mental illness. The loss of employment brings with it not only economic repercussions but a number of social and psychological ones as well: loss of self esteem and identity, lack of structure and purpose in life and reduced contacts with friends and former workmates. Although the picture is by no means a clear one there is evidence (Vigderhaus and Fishman, 1978) to suggest that job-loss may give rise to psychiatric disorder and even suicidal behaviour.

Employment is, we believe, such an important factor for both client and family that some specialisation within the social work team should be encouraged. This would enable one social worker to develop contacts with local employers and act as a resource about employment matters to the rest of the team. Face-to-face work with employers may be necessary not only to secure employment for a client, but also where necessary and with the client's permission, to allay some of the stereotyped ideas about mental illness that the employer may hold.

The government has a number of different schemes for the rehabilitation of handicapped people, and somebody with a psychiatric disorder may be eligible for help under these schemes. Rehabilitation units can teach new job-skills, encourage adaptations to a particular handicap and inculcate a regular work pattern. Disablement resettlement officers (DROs) are available to counsel those considering this step, and social workers should maintain close liaison with them. It may be that realistically a full-time job, on the open market, is not possible. In such cases a number of alternatives such as sheltered workshops and day centres may have to be considered.

Closely linked to the question of employment is that of *income maintenance*. For many people the maze of financial benefits and welfare entitlements is bewildering. This bewilderment may be compounded and complicated by mental illness. There is little evidence that social workers, as a group, are very effective at giving counsel with regard to the intricacies of the social security system. It may be that, having established the need for financial guidance and assistance, the best step a social worker can take is to call upon a specialist agency such as a welfare rights centre or a law centre. A citizens advice bureau may also be of use. Some social services departments do employ specialist welfare rights workers, in which case the social worker may refer to a colleague. However, most non-specialist social workers find it difficult to keep up-to-date with the changes in legislation and scales of financial entitlement and so should be wary of offering direct advice except in the most straightforward of cases.

The next important factor is one of *accommodation*, although this is clearly related to finance since even claiming supplementary benefit is easier with a permanent address. Many long-term psychiatric patients either have no family, or have lost contact with it. Discharge from hospital usually begins with looking for somewhere to live in such circumstances. For those people with an intact family a return home may not always be the best answer to their particular problems as we make clear in Chapter 6 with reference to the work of Vaughn and Leff (1976). Their work is a salutory example to those people who automatically think that a discharge back home is always the best solution to an accommodation problem.

Whilst Wing and Brown (1970) have indicated what damage poor institutional care may do to somebody suffering a mental illness, discharge into the community is not an easy solution. Too often many of the former chronic patients, when discharged, appear to drift into a dreary round of Salvation Army hostels, night-shelters and periods of sleeping rough (Leach and Wing, 1979). Alternatives to this grim prospect are available; but too often in short supply. Both hostels and group homes have their advocates as well as their critics (see Apte (1968) and Pritlove (1976)). One of the problems about both these alternatives is that they may begin to resemble the institutions they were designed to replace. One writer has aptly coined the phrase 'chronic wards in the community' to describe this phenomenon in some of the less stimulating hostels. Other alternatives which have been less widely explored are boarding-out schemes, where ex-patients live in ordinary domestic housing with a family to whom they are not related (sometimes termed 'substitute family care') (Olsen, 1979), and sheltered housing more commonly associated with the elderly (Butler, Oldman and Greve, 1983).

Finding somewhere appropriate for somebody to live and then supporting them during the period of adjustment is demanding work. A number of voluntary organisations such as the Richmond Fellowship, local groups of MIND and others have been instrumental in championing alternatives to hospital care. Social workers should seek to develop links with such groups in their own area. Indeed, some social workers find that working as a volunteer for such organisations provides them with a valuable stimulus and a pleasant change from battling with the bureaucracy of their employing department. Increasing use is also being made of self-help groups to enable people to come to terms with living in the community (Wing, 1975). A social worker may act as a catalyst to the development of such groups, putting people in touch with each other, providing accommodation and other assistance as and when required.

Physical needs

It is often forgotten by social workers that clients have physical as well as emotional needs and problems. In the mind-body equation too much attention tends to be given to the former and too little to the latter. In Chapter 7 we describe some of the physical treatments commonly used in psychiatry together with some of their possible side-effects. The social worker may have an important role to play here. Both client and family may have certain preconceptions, both negative and positive, about treatment which may need to be corrected. They may hold unrealistic fears about the treatment or unrealistic hopes for its success. The social worker may be in a better position than some of the medical personnel, to see how the client is reacting to the medication in the more natural setting of the home and what, if any, side-effects are being experienced. Again the social worker may have to act as an information-gatherer as well as giver.

It must be acknowledged that social workers receive very little instruction during their training about how the body functions, yet many will have to work alongside doctors and para-medics such as community psychiatric nurses, health visitors, and so on. A degree of humility on the part of the social worker in accepting this fact may facilitate communication and enhance team work.

The impact upon the social worker

Social workers are not immune from the widely held stereotypes of the mentally ill. They may be just as fearful and uneasy about dealing with mental illness as are many of the general public. And yet in the course of their work, they will be called upon to talk with and assist many people who are either formally diagnosed as mentally ill or who show signs of mental distress as part of some other problem.

It is here that adequate training and supervision become necessary. We have commented elsewhere (Pritchard and Butler, 1976) about the need for specialist training for those social workers who deal regularly with the mentally ill. The recent changes in the mental health legislation (see Chapter 10) now make it seem more likely that social services departments will pay more attention to this task than many have done in the past. However, this must be backed up by regular supervision so that the social worker is encouraged to examine his or her own responses to situations and some self-awareness developed.

Paul Brearley (1982) has written perceptively about the concept of risk in social work. This is something that as practioners we must all learn to live with. Nevertheless, reasonable apprehensions about professional competence can so easily be amplified into unmanageable proportions if the worker has not learned to recognise and come to terms with his own culturally induced fears and prejudices about the mentally ill.

So far in this section we have only addressed the problem of stress potentially induced by the client who is mentally ill. However, the social worker has also to deal with a number of other pressures from other sources. The social worker has to perform a number of different roles as the following diagram indicates (Figure 2.2).

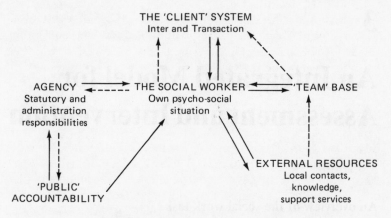

Figure 2.2 *Multiple social work roles*

The general public, for example, may have unrealistic ideas about how social workers can deal with certain mental health problems. There is often the expectation that a social worker will arrange a hospital admission at the first signs of distress and the social worker may have to resist pressure from the family to do so. Similarly, the local hospital may be making conflicting demands by expecting the social worker to arrange a discharge quickly and find accommodation for an ex-patient in an unrealistic period of time. The social worker may also be subject to a variety of agencies' pressures. Holding the balance between these sometimes competing forces is often essential if the best interests of the client are to be served. The social worker may have to resist demands which are made out of the desire for administrative tidiness or bureaucratic self-defensiveness.

3

An Integrated Model for Assessment and Intervention

An overview of the social work task

In the previous chapter we considered in broad terms the impact that mental disorder has upon the client, his family and the social worker. We have noted that mental illness disrupts communication pathways between people and that therefore this disturbs and distorts the psychological and social relationships of all involved.

The tasks for the social worker are, therefore, to assist in clarifying this distorted communication, to aid in the rehabilitation of family relationships and to seek to re-establish or support the optimum social functioning of client and family. In order to do this the social worker needs first to be able to engender a good working relationship. The basis for this, which is common to all social work settings, should be the ability to demonstrate to the client feelings of empathy, genuineness and warmth. This involves careful and concentrated listening, an acceptance of what is said and expressions of concern. These basic skills are really the bedrock upon which many more sophisticated verbal interventions are based, as Truax and Carkhuff (1967) have made clear in their research. As a model for his basic approach we would recommend readers to the works of Carl Rogers (1961). Over and above this there are three simple basic guides to social work with the mentally ill.

First, the social worker needs to sustain as much reality-based communication as possible. The social worker *must focus upon the here and now* and avoid being drawn into any discussion of bizarre or delusional material. No attempt should be made to 'humour' the client, but simple neutral responses offered. Second, because the client's perception may be disrupted, the social worker needs to *pace* intervention and communication at a speed which client and family can comprehend. This usually means that the social worker may need to speak more slowly, in a quiet and calm manner. Third, at all times, the social worker should be conscious of the potential strengths that exist within client and family, as well as apparent weaknesses and areas of dysfunction. This is necessary in order to gain an over-all understanding of client and family psycho-socio-economic circumstances. In order to achieve this we now offer a model of assessment and intervention that is essentially eclectic in that it draws upon a number of schools and disciplines.

An integrated model of assessment and intervention

There has been an unfortunate, and in our view, sterile war between the claims of the ego-dynamic and behaviourist schools with regard to intervention with the mentally ill. We offer an integrated model which draws upon both approaches. We have found elements in both that are helpful to the client and our thinking has been strongly influenced by a number of research studies which indicate the merits of this. Any intervention with vulnerable and troubled people should have, as its basis, some scientific evidence. We review some of this evidence later in Chapter 4.

Assessment

In an attempt to develop a practical method of work with the mentally ill we recognise that in order to communicate with a client we required a model of assessment that would specifically aid us in understanding their inner psychic experience. The approach that we favour is influenced by Bellak, who comes from the ego-dynamic school. He compares and contrasts the normal functioning of the person's self or ego, with that of the destructive effects of mental illness upon the individual's ego. As social workers our main concern is not with the cause of the mental illness, but its effects. This 'intra-psychic assessment' enables one to identify the specific areas of inter-personal disruption more clearly, and note more readily the problems that result from the ensuing disturbance. In Bellak's original work (1958) he outlined areas of ego-functioning and noted how typically these may be disrupted by mental illness. We have slightly modified this model in Table 4.1. We then follow this with a brief summary of ego-function and dysfunction in order to illustrate the possible effect of a disorder upon a clients' inner psychic experience.

Disruption of cognitive abilities

The impairment of a person's ability to 'think straight' is mentioned by all the different psychiatric schools and some might argue that all the subsequent affective responses come from this core disruption. The client's thoughts can become so disorganised that he may sometimes feel that his thoughts are out of control. Sometimes he feels that his ideas are alien in that they belong to someone else or that his thoughts feel speeded up or slowed down. This may result in perception or interpretation of events becoming badly skewed so that the client's self-image and self-esteem may also be disturbed. Resultant upon this type of disruption would be the characteristic response of the client who appears confused, distressed and seeking to withdraw from other people.

Disruption of psycho-social defences

The disruption of the client's psycho-social defences may cause his normal defensive technique either to become extremely rigid, even in response to minimal stress or to become erratic as they are overwhelmed by internal or external stimulus. This results in a highly vulnerable person whose threshold to psychic pain is seriously reduced. Perhaps the most common response is a rigidity of defences which leads to the client responding in a highly guarded manner. The feeling that his ego-defences are inadequate may tend to increase the likelihood of his withdrawal from inter-personal contact.

Table 3.1 *Intra-psychic assessment*

	Normal functioning (ego responsibilities)	*Disrupted functioning (ego responsibilities)* (N.B. specific effects dependent upon pattern of psychiatric disorder.)
Cognition	Thinking ability, perception and interpretation of events and self-image and self-esteem	Disturbance of thought patterns, perception and self-image and self-esteem
Psychosocial defences	Adaption mechanism to protect against internal and external stress, e.g. denial, rationalisation, projection	Defence becomes disturbed; this may result in their being used inappropriately, overly used, applied too rigidly, or failing to operate leaving the person abnormally vulnerable to stress
Control of drives	Control of basic drives -- sexual, aggression	Disruption of defences leaves person in fear of loss of control and open to fear of impulsive behaviour
Reality testing	Ability to differentiate between fantasy and reality, and to be aware of boundaries of own personality	Weakened ability to know real from unreal; unsureness of own identity and ego-boundary
Emotions	Appropriate mood response to internal and external situation	Inappropriate affective response to internal and external pressures. Ranges from apparent lack of emotion to excessive emotionality
Synthesis of experience	Ability to relate world and experience to concept of continuing integrity of self	Breakdown of awareness of self in psychic and social space, disruption of sense of integrity of self

Source: Adapted from Bellak (1958).

Disruption of control of drives

Closely associated with disturbance of psycho-social defences, is a threatened disruption of the client's ability to control his basic drives. In extreme cases this may be presented as inappropriate or impulsive behaviour. The fear is one of losing control as impulsive and aggressive emotions well up. Some of these feelings may be directed 'against-the-self', in which case self-harm becomes the concern, or outwards against others. The actual physical threat to other people is usually slight, but the fear of being overwhelmed is very disturbing to the individual who harbours the thoughts.

Disruption of reality-testing ability

In severe mental illness a disruption in the ability to differentiate between reality and imagery can create extreme confusion and distress. The client appears to be unsure of his psychic boundaries, and in grave episodes may be unaware of what is real and unreal, even to the extent of being uncertain about his own and others' psychic identity. He may be confused as to whom he is speaking and whether his thoughts are shared and known to those around him. The uncertainty about what is real and unreal threatens his core-identity and when this occurs he often emotionally opts out, as he seeks to avoid emotional stimulus that may threaten his precarious equilibrium.

Disturbance of emotions

The disturbance of emotions, or *affect*, can range from extreme excitement and elation to profound depression and despair. There may sometimes be a rapid change in the emotion for no apparent reason. As the client's emotions are distorted he often has difficulties in responding appropriately in inter-personal relationships, particularly those with whom he is most closely involved. This has important practical significance when it comes to creating a therapeutic working relationship. In two of the major psychiatric conditions, the schizophrenias and depression, there are often archetypal emotional responses. These are often described by experienced therapists as being all-pervasive. In the schizophrenias there appears to be a flattening and dulling of the emotional responses and within depression, a pervading sense of misery and despair. In both of these syndromes the prevailing affect may be reflected on to the social worker who may find himself drawn, by these emotional cross-currents, into the client's emotional world.

Disturbance of ability to synthesise and integrate experience

The impairment of the client's ability to synthesise in an integrated way his psycho-social experience leads to a sense of fragmentation of identity. Thus, with caution, the idea of schizophrenia being described as 'a split ego' can be a useful one. This fragmentation experience may well account for the apparent islets of normality. In all the main psychiatric syndromes, this synthesising ability is affected in different ways, but the common feature is disruption of the person's sense of self, which results in a severe undermining of the client's self-confidence and self-esteeem.

The social history

Our assessment model does not negate the need for a more formal social enquiry report or 'social history'. Indeed, colleagues and other agencies may expect that certain background social information is routinely gathered and collected. We have included an outline for such a report in Appendix I. However, we would urge a note of caution. Material such as a social history might contain needs to be gathered slowly. Any attempt to rush in at the moment of crisis to gather information for its own sake may be counter-productive and also, we suggest, not very accurate. Assessment, of whatever kind, is only the start of any work with someone who is mentally ill. For a model of intervention we have drawn heavily upon the work of the behaviourist, Arnold Lazarus.

This assessment model provides an understanding and entry into the distorted inner psychic world of mentally ill people which is not intrusive. Its advantage is that it primarily depends upon what the social worker observes and allows the social worker to respond to the client at his own pace. As the social worker can avoid an interrogative role, this facilitates the development of a sympathetic and understanding relationship.

A model of psycho-social intervention

Lazarus (1976), whilst trained as a behavioural psychologist, is essentially a pragmatist; he stressed that he is not concerned with epistomological questions, but rather with what works for the client. His aim is first to make an accurate assessment, then to define clearly what the presenting problems are; next, to examine which of the problems are capable of resolution and then as economically as possible to find some solution. Whilst utilising some behavioural techniques he insists that the work must be conducted within the context of a sustained relationship.

Social work readers in Britain may not be very familiar with Lazurus's work and it is therefore necessary to offer an introduction to his way of working. Lazarus suggests that it is useful to conceive of the individual as having a number of different areas in his life. He terms these 'modalities', and identifies the seven key modalities for dealing with the mentally ill as:

(a) Behaviour
(b) Affect
(c) Sensory
(d) Imagery
(e) Cognition
(f) Inter-personal relationships
(g) Drugs.

This gives rise to the mnemonic BASIC ID, which Freudians might view as a behaviourist's little joke. We think this list of modalities may be usefully extended, and propose that the concept of *defences* be incorporated as well as a modality that we will call *social*. This enables us to take in any ethnic or cultural dimensions to the case.

It is important to stress that in separating out these modalities we are only trying to disentangle what is clearly a complex inter-related system. The aim is to arrive, with the co-operation of the client, at a list of problems which may

Table 3.2 *Psycho-social intervention*

	Assessed Problem	*Possible Intervention Techniques* N.B. First create appropriate rapport.
Behaviour	Client complains of excessive shyness and feels he cannot cope with relationships and work	Assertive techniques. Counselling and positive relationships to improve confidence
Affect	Complains of feeling miserable	Supportive relationship (N.B. Other techniques under other modalities, e.g. psychotropic drugs)
Sensory	Feels physically tense, headaches, nausea	Ensure, via clients own doctor, that nothing is physically wrong – offer relaxation techniques and introduce to bio-feedback*
Imagery	Complains of worrying about work and visualises himself being dismissed	Counselling and rehearsal techniques to correct visual imagery
Cognition	Believes himself to be unattractive to other people, has low self-esteem	Explain his poor view of himself is in response to his problem (? depression)
Inter-personal relationships	Withdrawn and anxious with family and others	Counselling, possible use of type of con-joint (family) therapy. Teach social skills if necessary

(Table 3.2 *cont.* next page.)

* Bio-feedback is a technique whereby somebody learns to control certain body functions, such as heart rate and muscle tension, by means of self-monitoring. It is used by psychologists to enable people to control conditions such as anxiety.

Table 3.2 *cont.*

	Assessed Problem	Possible Intervention Techniques N.B. First create appropriate rapport.
Drugs	Consider other treatments – can any of the problems in modalities be attributable to 'drugs' or 'drink'?	Check out other treatments/agencies, monitor any use of chemotherapy, possible liaison with clients doctor for appropriate use of drugs, e.g. anti-depressants, sedatives
Defences	Withdrawn, emotionally flat, self-blaming (agression against self)	Counselling, explain to others the rationale for possible defensive withdrawal (improve cognition by positive reassurance to aid in lessening self-denigration)
Social	Lost time off work, resulting financial difficulties such as failing to organise sick-benefit claim	Ensure sick-benefits, arrange home visits to reduce travel costs, check mortgage/rent payments, etc., liaise as appropriate

then, still with the help of the client, be assigned some priority. The therapist then has the job of focusing upon specifically itemised tasks in the various modalities, and trying to marshall appropriate interventive techniques. This part of the work should be familiar to those social workers who have made use of a task-centred model.

In order to illustrate the practical use of the modalities we have outlined a psycho-social intervention with a client suffering from mild depression. This case illustration, whilst necessarily schematic, nevertheless offers an indication of the specific problems that need attention. The model may also be adapted to examine and support other members of the client's family. See Table 3.2.

The combined use of the intra-psychic assessment with the BASIC ID (DS) Model equips the worker with an approach that can help him to appreciate the four important elements to which we referred earlier:

(a) the unique situation of the client
(b) the characteristic form and content of the individual client's mental disorder
(c) the client's strengths as well as his weaknesses, as he attempts to attain as normal an adjustment as possible
(d) the meaning which the situation has for the individual client and his family.

In an earlier chapter we commented upon the need for the social worker to respond comprehensively to the client's psycho-social requirements. Such a response demands from the social worker the ability to undertake various roles and tasks, not only with the client and family but also with the wider community. Space precludes specific discussion, but the concepts found in Baker's *The Interpersonal Process in Generic Social Work* (1976) and Martin Davies's *The Essential Social Worker* (1981) provide complementary and useful practical guidelines. In particular Davies writes about practice know-how and highlights the importance of organising priorities. His book is of particular relevance to work with the chronically mentally disabled, because he advances the concept of a maintenance role for the social worker. Both authors adopt something of an eclectic stance and provide a useful foundation for basic social work practice.

One of the themes of our text is that social work as a profession should be eclectic in its search for theory and knowledge. Social workers must then forge out of this an integrated and effective practice. Social workers should be pragmatic, seeking out the best method for particular clients. However, as a profession we have been slow to evaluate the impact of our work. In the next chapter we review some of those studies (many drawn from outside social work) which indicate that effective interventions can be made with mentally ill people using techniques which are available to the social worker.

4

Research Foundations for the Integrated Approach

In the previous chapter we outlined an assessment and intervention model which sought to integrate concepts and techniques from the behavioural and ego-dynamic schools. In this chapter we intend to review a number of evaluatory studies that indicate the effectiveness of interventions with the mentally ill involving social work or related techniques.

The review is not definitive, but it draws upon a number of studies with which the busy social work practitioner may be unfamiliar. We have included studies from related disciplines where the techniques adopted are compatible with those of a social worker. We believe, as does Wing (1978), that at least three inter-related disciplines are concerned with interventions for the mentally ill: the social, psychological and medical. A multi-disciplinary approach, able to call upon these, and blend them to suit the particular individual client's requirements, stands the best chance of success. This requires that the social worker be both familiar with research and findings in other fields and discriminating in applying them to individual clients.

The psycho-neuroses

We will begin by reviewing three studies from different theoretical approaches, which have shown positive results in people with moderate or severe neurotic problems. It might be thought that clients with neurotic problems are of only marginal interest to social workers, but recent evidence (Huxley and Fitzpatrick 1983) suggests that there are a significant number of social service department clients who suffer from minor mental disorder.

The first study, conducted by Ginsberg and Marks (1977), explored the use of specially trained nurse-therapists who worked with neurotic patients. The therapists were given a short course in the use of simple behavioural techniques. As part of the study the authors also carried out a cost–benefit analysis of the project.

Over a period of one year, 191 patients were assessed for possible treatment with a behavioural method; 41 were excluded, as being unsuitable for the treatment, and following further drop out 87 patients were finally selected for treatment. At follow-up the researchers had complete data on 42 patients. The below 50 per cent follow-up, which resulted from tracing problems and incomplete data, is the major weakness of the study. However, it merits our attention because of its internal coherence and validity. Results were obtained by examining the self-reporting of patients and the assessments of the therapists. A sub-sample was also evaluated by an independent assessor and later, at the end of the follow-up period, clients in this sub-sample were interviewed by an independent researcher. The majority of the patients, 36, had phobic conditions, mainly agoraphobia and specific social phobias, while three others had obsesssive compulsive difficulties. These conditions, as we indicated earlier, can be very disabling and have serious implications for clients and their families.

The results were impressive: all showed a statistically significant improvement on measures of fear, general neurotic symptoms, free-floating anxiety, depressive feelings, lack of energy and vigour, confusion and tension levels. It was also noted that the treatment time required to reduce these levels of disturbance was positively correlated with the levels of original tension in the patients. Other important areas of improvement were noted, such as increased leisure activities, ability to handle work (in particular housework) and a reduction in the use of other health services. A greater degree of freedom was also experienced by relatives of the patients, so that both patient's and relatives' absence from work was reduced and earnings increased.

The researchers then undertook a cost-benefit analysis, comparing the actual cost of the treatment (including the training of nurses) with the apparent benefits gained, and offered monetary estimates of the effectiveness. The calculations indicated that not only was the intervention effective but it was also economical to implement. Ginsberg & Marks were able to show that nurse-therapists achieved results comparable with those obtained by psychiatrists and psychologists, whose training, of course, is more expensive than that of the nurses.

Many other psychologists are prepared to share their techniques with others. However, social workers in this country, unlike their counterparts in the United States, have been slow to adopt their methods. Within the past ten years there have been a few indications that the value of a behavioural approach, within a framework of social work, is becoming more accepted (Jehu *et al.*, 1972; Hudson, 1974; Jones and Pritchard, 1980).

In complete contrast, Siassi (1979) using a psychoanalytically based form of intervention demonstrated that neurotic patients, drawn predominantly from lower socio-economic groups, could be helped. He used psychiatrists, psychologists and social workers as treatment agents, and in a controlled trial of some two years demonstrated by means of the Hamilton anxiety-rating scale (1959) the effectiveness of his approach. Whilst his sample was small in numbers the importance of this study lies in the type of client helped. Working-class clients may be denied psycho-therapeutic help because of their apparent lack of verbal skills and yet they form the majority of social workers' clientele.

The third study in this section, by Cooper *et al.* (1975), is probably better known. They evaluated the care given by routine family practitioner services to chronically neurotic people and compared it with an experimental service, in which social workers were attached to group practices. The samples consisted of people with a chronic neurotic condition of at least twelve months standing. The main problems appeared to be morbid anxiety and depression. The research was designed as a controlled trial: the prevailing service provided by the GP being compared with a similar service enhanced by the provision of a social worker attached to the practice. Patients were assessed at the beginning of the project and again after the follow-up period, on standardised social assessment scales and a standardised psychiatric interview. There was a good patient response, both initially and at follow-up. Over 80 per cent of experimental and control patients were assessed after one year, yielding 92 patients in the experimental group and 97 in the control group. There was a broad similarity at the outset between the physical and psychiatric states of the two groups, though of course it was not possible to match them exactly, and there were slight, but not statistically significant, differences in social characteristics. With regard to psychiatric disturbance the experimental group had a greater number of depressive people though the control group had a slightly larger number of people described as endogenously depressed — 11 per cent as compared with 2 per cent. In both groups the main complaint was one of chronic anxiety, this being so in about half of the cases.

The results of the study are both interesting and encouraging. It was found that both groups of patients required psychotropic drugs for six months or more after the initial treatment, though in all instances those in the experimental group required them for less time than those in the control group. Next, the experimental group of patients used other psychiatric services far less — only 5 per cent were later referred to psychiatric services compared with nearly 16 per cent of the control group. Furthermore, only 30 per cent of these patients were in touch with any other social agency as compared with 40 per cent of the control group. The psychological functioning and social adjustment scores also showed that the improvements were greater in the experimental group. While both groups of patients were considered to need further support, the balance was again in favour of the social-worker-attached group.

The implications of this study, in which social workers took the major role, are threefold: first, people who were offered social work help in addition to the family practitioner's care showed the greater improvement; secondly, they needed less 'expensive' services subsequently, and thirdly, it adds weight to the belief that social workers can work successfully alongside family practitioners (Pritchard and King, 1980).

Social and psychological intervention with depressed people

In chapter 1 we described the commonly accepted signs of depression and indicated the impact that the disorder may have upon the individual and his family. Many social service department clients arrive with feelings of helplessness and low self-esteem either as a primary cause for their referral or as a reaction to one or other of the problems that has brought them into the social work network. For example Hawton and Roberts (1981) have pointed to the possible links between such feelings of hopelessness and potential child abuse.

In recent years psychologists have added to our understanding of depressive feelings and produced some effective interventive measures to counter them. For example, Seligman (1975) bases his theory upon the idea that helplessness, as a state, is a learned response whilst for Beck (1967, 1979) the depressed individual's use of language is indicative of a low self-image. The depressed person's gloomy view of himself becomes self-reinforcing, leading to a further sense of defeat and failure, which in turn contributes to the feeling of inadequacy and unworthiness. The treatment of depression, has traditionally been by means of drugs or ECT (see Chapter 7), but over the last decade increasing use has been made of a combined approach, that is, combining anti-depressant drugs with various psychological and social therapies. One of the early examples of this was described by Weissman (1974), who used social workers acting as social therapists specifically aiming to improve the social adjustment of the depressed clients. When social therapy was given in conjunction with psychotropic drugs, it was found that those clients receiving help from both social workers and anti-depressant drugs, were on a whole range of measures, markedly more improved after a year than people receiving a placebo (a chemically inactive substance) or just the anti-depressant drug on its own. The finding that combined therapy was more efficacious than drugs or psychotherapy singly has been supported by a number of further studies undertaken by Weissman and her team (1981).

Much of the work in this area has been carried out in the United States but a British study of particular interest was undertaken by Blackburn (1981), a psychologist, whose team included psychiatrists. They replicated the important work of Rush *et al.* (1977) which sought to evaluate a combined cognitive therapy and pharmaco-therapy approach. The Rush study had demonstrated the benefits of cognitive therapy (see p. 71) together with anti-depressants as distinct from psycho-therapy or drugs alone. In view of the well-established work that demonstrated that tricyclic anti-depressant drugs are superior to a placebo (see Chapter 7 and Appendix II), the Blackburn team did not use a placebo in their study. They compared two samples of patients, the first drawn from a hospital out-patient clinic and the other from a general practice, treated by three randomly allocated forms of intervention: drugs alone, cognitive therapy alone and a combined treatment of cognitive therapy and drugs. In selecting clients, very strict criteria were applied with regard to their depressive symptoms and a number of standardised tests were used to establish these. From an initial sample of 140 patients, (71 hospital out-patients and 69 from a general practice), some patients considered unsuitable were excluded, yielding a final sample of 40 hospital out-patients and 24 from the general practice. There were few socio-economic differences in the two samples, which contained a similar proportion to people with suicidal ideas and behaviour (55 per cent and 45 per cent respectively). Treatments lasted between twelve and sixteen weeks for all three forms of intervention.

Two internationally recognised and standardised rating scales for depression were used — those of Beck *et al.* (1961) and Hamilton (1960). In addition, a scale devised by Snaith *et al.* (1978) was used to assess irritability, depression and anxiety. Thus, clear baselines of depression and anxiety were established. Blackburn and his colleagues were concerned to examine changes to those baselines and indicated their treatment results in terms of the percentage of change.

In brief, those patients given the combination of drugs and cognitive therapy did better than those receiving only one or the other. However, the group receiving cognitive therapy alone was found to have better results than those in the general practitioner's group who were only having drugs. The author's, however, did query whether the general practitioner's patients took all their medication as prescribed in the group that was only having drugs.

Another British study of particular relevance to social workers was undertaken by Jane Gibbons and her colleagues 1978, 1979). This study evaluated a social work service for patients who had deliberately taken poison. This is described more fully in Chapter 9. Here we will only briefly mention part of their results which are appropriate to this section. One of the great merits of the Gibbons study was its experimental design. It supports the conclusions of a number of writers already mentioned, that a social work intervention can improve depressed clients' state of well-being, lessen the need for other, sometimes more expensive, services, and improve the client's social functioning. The studies of Cooper (1975), Weissman (1974) and Gibbons (1978, 1979) provide some indication that social work has a contribution to make to an effective prevention programme.

To summarise, there is good evidence to indicate that when drugs are used appropriately and backed up by adequate and purposive social and psychological treatment, the results are better than if these interventions are made singly. The social worker must be willing to learn from other professions and work with them for the general good of the patient or client suffering from depression.

Intervention with people with schizophrenia

We have already acknowledged in Chapter 1 that the aetiology of schizophrenia is complicated and surrounded in controversy. Peter Sedgwick (1982) has effectively demolished some of the myths that have been erected around this disorder and in passing, pointed to the unfortunate fact that

parents are often quite unreasonably blamed for having
created the disorder in their child. The burden of guilt carried
by many parents and to an extent amplified by the actions
and attitudes of some social workers, may now subside a
little. What is becoming clear, however, is that patient —
family interactions may affect the progress of people with
schizophrenia (Greenley, 1979; Brown *et al.*, 1972) and that
this interaction plays an important part in the referral
(Leon and Micklin, 1978).

Indirect intervention

In order to examine the link between the family and the
client's progress Goldstein (1974) focused upon social work
intervention with the *parents* of young in-patients. She
looked at 30 consecutive hospital admissions of people diagnosed as suffering from schizophrenia. In order to meet her
criteria they had to be single, aged between 17 and 33, and
living with their parents prior to their admission to hospital.
She tried to establish whether parental attitudes were related
to the outcome of the treatment; whether social work involvement could change parental attitudes, and the extent to
which there was any link between a change in parental
responses and the outcome of psychiatric hospital treatment
for the client. Despite some methodological problems she
found four significant changes related to patient progress.
First, an improved attitude of parents towards the decision
to admit the patient to hospital; second, an improvement in
parents' expectations and tolerance of the patient; third,
improvements in the quality of patient and parent relationships, with parents becoming more willing to be involved in
the whole treatment process. Finally, although not reaching
a level of statistical significance, there was some indication
of positive changes in the quality of the parents' marital
relationships. This study is a useful pointer towards a preventive model for this kind of patient — family situation,
particularly when one reflects upon the pressures born by all
in the families of people suffering from schizophrenia, as
Creer has demonstrated (Creer 1975).

Direct intervention

There are a number of different treatment models for direct
work with people who have schizophrenia. We will briefly
explore three broad approaches which are of relevance to
social work.

The first is from the *behavioural school* and was an early
example of operant conditioning for chronic schizophrenics.
It demonstrated some of the problems to be overcome in
dealing with severely institutionalised people (Baker, 1971).
Baker took a small group of patients in a traditional back
ward of a large county hospital, aged between 27 and 69
(average 53 years) who had not spoken for three or more
years. While the range for mutism was three to 37 years, the
average was 22 years. The patients' daunting length of stay
in hospital ranged from 16 to 42 years, with an average of
29 years. The researchers introduced a 'token economy'
scheme which sought to reinforce all positive social behaviour
and in particular, to encourage speech and interaction with
other people. Patients acting in the approved way were
'rewarded' with a small token which might be exchanged
for food or cigarettes. The results were impressive. All the
experimental patients improved, though it should be noted
that Baker recognised the social impact which the project
had upon ward staff. He acknowledged that a 'continuously
present emotional warmth from the therapist appeared to be
an important prerequisite for successful conditioning'. Thus
in effect the project had not only improved the quality of
speech of the patients and their interaction but had also
changed the spirit of the ward. A finding similar to this was
noted in a separate study by Stoffelmayr *et al.* (1979) who
used the 'token economy' approach, along with social
therapy in the treatment of longstanding schizophrenic
patients. It was found that in addition to changes in the
patients, there were marked improvements in staff attitudes.
This form of behavioural intervention has important
implications, not least of which are certain ethical questions.
Nonetheless, these techniques could provide part of the
therapeutic armoury for social work with chronically
institutionalised people.

Another approach which illustrated the growth of eclecticism and the integration of methods was the use of *psychotropic drugs* with one of the verbal therapies. A study by Goldberg *et al.* (1977) looked at 104 young acute patients who were randomly assigned to four after-care programmes, with high and low dosage of drugs with either family therapy or no family therapy (a short outline of the use of family therapy is given in the next chapter). In brief, the best results were obtained where a low dosage of drugs was combined with family therapy. These results were still evident at the six-month follow-up.

In a similar study, which included a double blind drug trial in the methodology, Hogarty *et al.* (1979) examined the use of social therapy with combinations of fluphenazine, given either as an injection or by the mouth, and the use of placebos. Hogarty compared the different treatment permutations and again confirmed that there were longer-lasting benefits where social therapy was offered in conjuction with medication. There was also an indication that the social therapy helped to maintain the patient on a lower level of psychotropic drugs.

A particularly impressive piece of work from Sweden was concerned with the long-term management of clients with schizophrenia (Lindberg, 1981). He reported on three related studies which used a combination of psychotherapies with depot neuroleptic drugs (see Chapter 7). In a carefully matched study of samples of young schizophrenics, he found quite clearly that groups having combined drugs and psychotherapy did significantly better than those on drugs alone or those receiving no treatment. In another survey, of people over the age of 40, Lindberg again found similar benefits from the combined approach though with less marked results. In a study of patients who had been ill for twelve or more years however, while the integrated approach reduced symptomatology and appeared to aid personality functioning, some of the emotional and social problems associated with chronic schizophrenia appeared to persist. What was clear is that, bearing in mind the longevity of the illness, Lindberg's sample was obviously functioning at a better level than would be expected in such a group of chronically disturbed people. An important aspect of this study was the eclecticism. As in the 'chronic' sample, a token economy method was used and was found to be particularly helpful.

No brief review can do justice to this important work, and readers are urged to explore this text for themselves.

In another comparable study from Sweden, the 'combined' approach was also used by Göttfries and Rüdeberg (1981). They examined the role of neuroleptics in an integrated treatment programme with people suffering from chronic schizophrenia. They reported on a series of related studies with the emphasis being upon appropriate drug treatment and pyschological and social functioning.

This work however had some methodological problems with regard to maintaining the number of patients at follow-up. Also their report appears to be less well translated and some issues are left unclear. Nevertheless, the feature to note was that in addition to the benefits gained from a combined approach, the older, more chronic patients found a behavioural approach very successful, as it appeared to break up unhelpful rigid routines. On the other hand, the younger, less institutionalised patients found the behavioural approach somewhat limited and complained that it appeared to be somewhat simplistic and childish. This latter group appeared to gain greater benefits from a more psychodynamically oriented intervention and valued the exploration of the patient—parent relationship.

At a follow-up five years after discharge, the results appeared to be very good and of the final 42 patients reported, over 30 per cent were functioning reasonably well — considerable achievements with such a group of people. A small cost—benefit analysis study had also been undertaken within the larger study and it was estimated that there were clear economic gains.

International comparisons are always difficult to draw but for European social workers the surveys of Lindberg and those of Gottfries and Rudeberg are of particular relevance because of their broadly shared cultural background. The latter authors concluded that hospital care for life-long sufferers of schizophrenia, is ten times as expensive as the equivalent care provided in the community and probably five times as costly if it is in permanent hostels. Nevertheless, they acknowledge the dangers inherent in an 'economic evaluation' alone. They stress that responsibility for the *quality* of a patient's life should not end with discharge from hospital, as it could easily degenerate into an impoverished existence. Given sufficient resources this can be avoided, as Olsen (1979) has already demonstrated in Britain.

Programmes based on community care

The work that we have cited so far has been mainly clinically based and has focused upon particular diagnostic groups and methods of intervention. However, there is good evidence of the efficacy of broadly-based community services for those who are mentally ill. This gives hope to those who wish to see our larger institutions further reduced in size.

Braun and his colleagues (1981), in a comprehensive review of projects designed to assist with the de-institutionalisation of chronic psychiatric patients, concluded that community-care programmes can cut down readmission rates, shorten the length of hospital stay and improve patients' social and psychological functioning. Readers will find Braun's review worthy of more detailed study.

One major work however warrants further amplification. Stein and Test (1980), in a work of particular methodological rigour, designed a community-based treatment programme (using all the disciplines, medicine, social work, nursing, etc.) as an alternative to in-patient care. Patients were randomly assigned to two treatment modalities: a 14-month intensive community treatment programme or a traditional mental hospital for as long as necessary. Comparisons of the results clearly showed that the community-care programme could be an effective alternative to hospital treatment for the large majority of the sample. Not only did people stay longer in the community but the quality of life, as demonstrated by levels of social adjustment, self-esteem, general satisfaction and overall improvement in functioning, was greatly improved.

However, one important caveat was that when the special treatment programme of support was stopped, the differences originally found between the two groups lessened and the gains previously obtained were lost; this echoes the studies from Sweden cited earlier which acknowledged the need for continued supportive services.

Of particular interest, in these cost-conscious times, was the cost–benefit analysis of the Stein and Test study conducted by Weisbrod (1980). As with the earlier cost–benefit study we cited (Ginsberg and Marks, 1977) it proved difficult to attach a monetary value to the various humanitarian aspects of the study such as the improved quality of life for those people who were maintained outside hospital. However, an attempt was made to cost the more tangible elements of the two alternatives. Initially it was found that the cost of community care was some 11 per cent higher than that for hospital-based care. But if a broader view were taken and a number of indirect costs and benefits included, such as the earnings of potential patients, lower financial costs to the patients' families, and the reduction in the use of other services, then the monetary gain was found to be in favour of the community-based programme.

Conclusion

We are aware that because of the need to compress a great deal of material into so short a space we are in danger of over-generalising. We have also had to omit mention of studies which have demonstrated the effectiveness of day-care services and self-help groups. However, we believe that from a survey of the literature, such as this, five general points emerge which are of importance to the social worker dealing with mentally ill patients.

(1) Behaviourally based treatments have proved to be particularly effective where clear and limited goals can be set. Their worth has been demonstrated in a number of residential settings, most notably token economy schemes with chronic schizophrenic patients, and by

means of reality-orientation techniques as part of the hospital care of patients suffering from senile dementia (Holden, 1982).

(2) Social work too has proved to be at its most effective when borrowing something from the behavioural school. In adopting a task-centred approach social workers are learning to set clear and limited goals for themselves and work within time limits.

(3) Psychologists also developed, by means of cognitive therapy, a treatment approach which offers hope for work with depressed patients. In the course of their work, social workers see many people who are depressed. Cognitive therapy techniques are readily assimilable into the social workers' style of work.

(4) A broadly based 'ego-dynamic' approach is helpful in ameliorating some family problems, and hence in assisting with the client's rehabilitation and adjustment.

(5) Drugs, when used appropriately and backed up by other forms of therapy have proven effectiveness with many types of disorder.

These general developments, as we have indicated earlier, have a number of implications for the social worker. They demonstrate that positive work with the mentally ill is possible, that one may intervene with a sense of optimism and that social work has a contribution to make. However, this requires that the social worker adopt a discriminating approach with regard to the type of intervention that is used matching this to the particular client's requirements. Furthermore, social workers must learn to borrow from other professional groups, particularly psychologists, and adapt some of their techniques to the social work model. Finally, a number of studies demonstrate that working as a therapeutic team enhances the treatment programme. Social workers must learn to co-operate with colleagues and contribute to this *team* approach.

5

Different Approaches to Work with Mentally Disordered People

Social casework is perhaps the most familiar method of intervention to social workers. However, it is only one of a number which rely upon some form of verbal interaction to bring about change within the client. Throughout this text we have advocated an eclectic approach – one which draws upon a number of influences for its strength. Lazarus, in his notion of multi-modal behaviour therapy, comes closest to our own thinking about interventive technique and practice. In this chapter we intend to explore some of the different therapeutic models which are available to the social worker. Some of them are drawn upon quite heavily in our eclectic model, and allusion to them is made else where in the text. The object of this chapter is not to pass on a set of techniques, but rather to indicate some of the identifying features of alternative therapies which may be followed up by interested readers.

Some of the approaches described may be readily incorporated by a social worker into his or her normal daily work. This will enable the social worker to offer a broader range of skills which may be used in a discriminating way. It may be that one of these techniques could be employed in joint work with a psychiatrist, psychologist or nurse with a selected group of clients. Even if the techniques are not employed directly, a knowledge of them will at least serve to inform readers of what colleagues may be doing in their own therapeutic work. Social workers should be encouraged to experiment and extend their skills. An interest in a specialised form of intervention may have all kinds of benefits – facilitating work with other disciplines; enabling the social worker to offer particular expertise to the social work team and improved job satisfaction. Anybody interested in working in these ways should look around for people with a similar interest. The next step may be to find a practitioner who is able to offer, albeit on an informal basis, some supervision or advice. In this way one session of group-work, or family therapy may be easily incorporated into a more traditional workload.

We have chosen to examine these other methods of therapy under six headings. This is somewhat arbitrary, since many share a common base and hence overlap to some extent. Similarly, confusion is sometimes created by the fact that some practitioners apply slightly different names to the work that they do. The therapies we propose to discuss are as follows:

(a) individual psychotherapy
(b) behavioural psychotherapy
(c) social skills training
(d) family therapy
(e) group psychotherapy
(f) existential therapy.

Individual psychotherapy

The basis of all forms of psychotherapy is that the relationship between the client and the therapist is the medium by which change can take place. Essentially the major task is the attempt, on both sides, to understand the meaning, for the client, of his problem.

Many different schools of psychotherapy exist. Some, such as followers of Freud, Jung or Klein, seek to bring about this understanding by offering to the client a particular view of the world, or the language in which to explain it. In essence they offer a framework for understanding human behaviour which the client is encouraged to borrow and use for himself. Others – usually followers of two American psychologists, Rogers and Kelly – lay the stress upon this understanding taking place within the client's own concepts and view of the world. They emphasise the importance of the therapist attempting to understand and empathise with what the client is really trying to communicate. On the other hand, followers of Freud, Jung or Klein tend to be more interventive and seek to offer an interpretation of the client's feelings and actions within their own theoretical model of human development.

The differences in the underlying attitudes are reflected in differences of technique. Those who look to European theoreticians for their inspiration tend to push the client into a personal exploration which may involve reflection upon and re-evaluation of earlier, usually childhood, experiences. Those who draw upon the work of later American theorists, concentrate upon a more supportive, less intensive type of relationship, which tends to give more attention to current, rather than to early experiences. The therapeutic effect is engendered with less emphasis upon the discovery of insight and more upon the supportive effects of the development of genuine understanding by the therapist, reduction of anxiety, and (where necessary) straightforward counselling about changes in daily life.

The nature of the contract may also vary between schools, although all tend to rely upon a client who is willing to work at, and spend some time upon the undertaking. Those who pursue insight usually envisage an open-ended commitment, or at least one running into many months or even years. Constraints upon time, and concern about possible diminishing returns, have encouraged other theorists to advocate time-limited contracts or so-called *focal psychotherapy*. This latter seeks to partialise problems and to deal with only some of them. This thinking has spilled over into casework with the notion of time-limited work espoused by Reid and Epstein (1972).

Criteria for selecting patients also vary from school to school, but most appear to favour the following:

(a) recognition of symptoms as psychological
(b) tendency to be introspective
(c) personal curiosity

(d) honesty in discussing difficulties
(e) willingness to experiment and change
(f) readiness to participate in possibly lengthy therapy sessions.

The actual process of therapy also varies from therapist to therapist and client to client. However, it is possible to make some generalisations and indicate some general points on which most therapists will reflect. The first concerns the foci of major anxiety within the client as reflected by what he says and how he says it. The questions addressed are:

1. How are the anxieties, which are displayed, related to experiences earlier in life and present day functioning?
2. How does the client tend to organise his talk?
3. How and why does he juxtapose topics, and jump from theme to theme?
4. Does the flow of talk suggest some underlying connection?
5. How are feelings expressed?
6. Do they appear to be distorted or exaggerated?
7. Are strongly held feelings displaced into activity or given symbolic representation?

In concentrating upon these and other issues it will be apparent that the actual presenting symptoms tend to slip somewhat into the background. This may appear baffling to the client whose immediate concern is usually the relief of some distressing symptom. To a greater or lesser degree this approach is true of all psychoanalytically based interventions, the implication being that the presenting symptom is merely a reflection of some underlying distress or trauma. It is argued by those who practice these methods that concentrating upon the overt symptoms might provide immediate relief, but would produce either a substitution of symptoms or even breakdown at some later date. This is a statement which would be disputed by those who advocate behaviourally-based treatments.

For a long time the effectiveness of such techniques has been under attack, particularly by those who advocate treatment based upon behaviourist principles. To some extent these battles have now died down, partly as the result of more sophisticated methods of evaluation on the part of those who advocate and practice psychotherapeutic techniques, also because many practitioners from the behavioural camp have begun to appreciate the importance of *the relationship* to their own therapeutic work. Many, formerly strict adherents to the behaviourist cause, now incorporate elements of psychotherapeutic technique into their practice, giving rise to yet another grouping – the behavioural psychotherapists.

Behavioural psychotherapy

This form of therapy relies largely for its rationale upon theories developed by psychologists interested in learning theories and animal behaviours. The techniques drawn from this theoretical work are then applied to clients within a framework which relies to a limited extent upon the ideas generated by the purely relationship-based therapies that we have already discussed. These latter theories are invoked since many have realised that 'helping' of any kind is difficult outside the context of a good relationship. The client must feel highly motivated, see the therapist as helpful and understanding and believe that the therapist is able to comprehend the full meaning of his difficulties.

Behavioural techniques tend to be applied to a fairly narrow range of psychiatric problems and only to be invoked when specific targets for change can be designated. Problems such as the following have been successfully tackled in this way:

(a) anxieties
(b) obsessive – complusive rituals
(c) some forms of sexual dysfunction such as impotence
(d) compulsive disorders such as gambling, obesity, anorexia and self-mutilation.

Large areas of the psychiatric pantheon, such as acute schizophrenia and severe depression are rarely approached in this way. Seligman who has advanced the idea of *learned helplessness* (Seligman, 1975), has demonstrated the possibility of working with depressed people and many of his ideas and techniques may be readily incorporated into social work. Beck *et al.* (1979) have concentrated upon the ways in which depressed patients think about and view the world. He describes their gloomy view of the world and the future as 'negative cognitive distortions'. What is required, he believes, is that by 'the application of logic and rules of evidence' the individual's information-processing be returned to reality. The cognitive therapy that he has evolved is an 'active, directive, time-limited and structured procedure based on the assumption that affect and behaviour are largely determined by the way we structure the world'. The techniques he employs are eminently suitable for use by social workers.

Within an institutional setting, rehabilitation programmes adopting a token economy system have been successful. These seek to reward or reinforce positive behaviour, such as self-care, by means of the staff distributing tokens to the ward population. Chronic long-stay patients, particularly those suffering the aftermath of schizophrenia, have been among those helped.

Isaac Marks (1975), a leading British behaviourist, has usefully divided the methods used into two broad types:

(a) those which reduce anxiety linked behaviour, such as phobias or compulsive rituals
(b) those which reduced appetitive behaviour such as exhibitionism and obesity.

Anxiety reduction usually relies upon some variant of exposure such as desensitisation or flooding. *Flooding* implies repeated exposure to anxiety — producing situations, with the expectation that gradually the sense of panic will decline. *Desensitisation* approaches the problem more gradually, exposing the client to the phobic object in a controlled or diluted format. This may be accompanied by reassurance or the application of various relaxation techniques. The objective is to enable the individual to confront the formerly phobic or anxiety-provoking situation or object in a calmer frame of mind, feeling that events remain under their control.

In the reduction of appetitive behaviour, techniques such as aversion, self-regulation and satiation are employed.

Aversion, as the word implies, relies upon developing an association between an unpleasant stimulus and the previously desirable object. Alcoholics, for example, may be presented with their favourite tipple and then made to feel unwell by the ingestion of a drug or by being presented with gross images of drunkenness. *Self-regulation* may be engendered by moral imprecation or by encouraging the individual to reflect upon the legal and other consequences of some act. This really seems to amount to little more than a mechanical exercising of the individual's embryonic conscience. *Satiation* implies encouraging an individual to enact repeatedly the behaviour which it is hoped to extinguish. Chain—smoking to the point of nausea or to a realisation that little satisfaction is being gained from each succeeding cigarette would be one example of the technique.

Advocates claim good results with these techniques, but not that they effect a 'cure' in the medical sense. Rather a new set of behaviours has been learned, which with practice will be retained. The individual is thus more able to cope with everyday life.

Social skills

The social-skills approach is based upon the belief that 'some forms of mental disorder are caused by or exacerbated by lack of social competence' (Trower *et al.*, 1978). This failure of social competence results in abnormal behaviour, and an inability to communicate with others. Such descriptions go wider than traditional psychiatric diagnosis and seek to focus upon those daily behaviours which make relationships with others difficult. Attention is paid to such factors as non-verbal behaviour, personal presentation in social situations and communication style. The intention is that by identifying these failings and using a variety of techniques to work on them the individual 'can be taught directly a new and more socially accepted repertoire of skills, which will enable them to influence their enviroment sufficiently to attain basic personal goals' (Trower *et al.*, 1978).

Some of the methods adopted rely upon newer techno-
logies such as videotape. For example, an individual's way
of presenting himself in a particular situation may be fed
back to him on television. Other methods adopt ploys, such
as role rehearsal, or role reversal, which have much in common
with the idea of psychodrama, associated with Moreno
(Moreno, 1934).

Goldsmith and McFall, quoted by Trower (1978), sum up
this approach 'in contrast to the therapies aimed primarily at
the elimination of "maladaptive" behaviours, skills training
emphasises the positive, educational aspects of treatment . . .
Whatever the origins of deficit (e.g. lack of experience,
faulty learning, biological dysfunction) it often may be overcome or partially compensated through appropriate training
in more skilful response alternatives'.

Evidence about the effectiveness of these methods appears
rather inconclusive although encouraging enough to suggest
the adoption of a broader and more extensive programme
with appropriate evaluation.

Family therapy

Family therapy is concerned with the conjoint interviewing
of natural groups — usually couples or families — with the
intention of intervening in the systems developed by these
intimate relationships, rather than upon an individual's
psychopathology. Practitioners vary in their techniques, but
most start with the referred client and then seek to set them,
for purposes of treatment, within the context of the nuclear
family. In some cases this may involve other members of the
extended family or relevant people in the wider social network.
In essence the approach relies upon the belief that an individual's presenting problem can only be understood and worked
upon as part of the total system generated by the communi-
cations and interactions of the family members. This would
mean that the concepts of the 'patient' as the locus of
the disturbance or disorder has no place in a genuine family
therapy approach.

This approach is used for a wide variety of presenting
problems particularly where difficulties in relationships,

control, awareness of personal boundaries, and separation are suspected. Different therapists call upon different theoretical bases for their work but most agree upon a number of factors which are seen to be efficacious. First, is the belief that the family itself is a resource for support and help to the individual. In many cases all that may be needed is a catalyst to unlock the helping processes. Second, is the belief that many disturbances result from poor or distorted patterns of communication within the family grouping. Help in examining intra-family communication and pointing out possible distortions may allow the family to express more freely feelings and emotions. Next comes the potential for the sharing of experiences and with it the reassertion of appropriate boundaries between the individuals. Personal feelings towards other members of the family become more open and personal autonomy may be reasserted.

Finally, helping the group to examine its own power-relationships may enable members to understand better the part which they, as individuals and as a collective, play in the promotion of stress and anger.

The therapist, or therapists, in these sessions may be subject to all kinds of pressures from the people involved and may need to exercise considerable power to maintain control and reflect the realities of the situation.

Sessions may involve some activity-based work. For example, role-playing exercises of various kinds may be adopted to enable participants to see a situation from a different perspective and rehearse alternative responses. Family sculpting is another technique sometimes used. This involves members of the family replaying a particular incident or upset that they have experienced, physically forming a group-pose and then examining this with the help of the therapist.

Outcome is difficult to measure in such cases since the effects are not focused upon one individual but have repercussions throughout the family and beyond. Those evaluative studies which have been attempted do not seem to indicate that improvement goes far beyond that recorded for the usual rates of spontaneous remission over a two-year period. However, what does emerge is the fact that change may occur very rapidly and it seems likely that the therapist can provide a kind of forcing-house atmosphere which brings about change more quickly and therefore more efficiently.

Group therapy

The term *group therapy* tends to be somewhat loosely used. On occasions it seems to be used as a euphemistic cloak to cover any activity which takes place in a group. Many activity-based or discussion groups seem to have taken on this title in order to legitimise their existence. These forms of grouping may be effective, within their own terms of reference, but we think the term *group therapy* should be confined to groups which are specifically brought together for the relief of illness or personal distress by means of an examination of the group-processes which are generated by that coming together. Individual tasks may be typified as the sharing of experiences, enhancement of the ability to communicate, a reduction of defences, and the completion of developmental tasks. The group leader should see his primary function as facilitating all or some of these tasks by fostering group interaction and encouraging the members to examine the processes which are going on around them and are instigated by their network of relationships.

Commonly such groups consist of about eight people and one, or two, group leaders. They usually meet for between one and two hours, on a weekly or twice-weekly basis. Some are intended to run for a limited number of sessions and typically do not admit new members. Others, particularly those based upon a ward or treatment unit, are ongoing and open-ended with new members joining as old ones leave.

Many practitioners go to great lengths to describe selection criteria and to outline the type of person they consider suitable for this kind of therapy. It is usually confined to those people with non-psychotic disorders, who are willing to examine their own ways of functioning and who will be strong enough to withstand the sometimes heightened emotions which may develop within the sessions. Yalom (1970) provides a fuller discussion of these points and is in our view the most reliable of the sources available.

As to what the leaders actually do in the sessions, opinions tend to fall along a continuum: at one end are leaders who believe in intervention and self-revelation; at the other, those who prefer to distance themselves from the group, and retain a certain diffidence about personal details. There seems little agreement among practitioners upon these and other points beyond the fact that it is the leaders' job to select the members and convene the meetings — this usually, in our experience, means arranging the chairs as well! Generally, individual members are encouraged to present their thoughts to the group. The leaders' task is to facilitate this and to help the group to examine both the content of the statements and the way in which as a collectivity, the group handles any particular situation. The therapeutic effects seem to vary from a simple form of social learning — presenting oneself in social situations, trying out one's social skills — to a cathartic relief at expressing oneself, and sharing previously harboured ideas with others who may also have them. The development of personal insight and self-awareness may also ensue.

As in most areas of verbal therapy, effectiveness is difficult to assess, although advocates of the technique have produced positive results, which at least seem to satisfy themselves. One bad reason for running groups is the rather glib assumption that it will somehow be economical. Social workers may sometimes be pushed unwillingly in this direction by those who argue that seeing eight alcoholics — or depressives or whatever — together is a better use of time than seeing individuals on their own. In practice this usually proves a false argument. Selection of members and their preparation for the group is time-consuming. Working in groups poses its own particular strains and may involve two workers *in tandem*. This in turn can create difficulties if the two leaders are not fully in tune with each other.

Existential therapies

In seeking to typify this final group of therapies we have chosen the term *existential*, although 'experimental' might equally apply. The term is meant to cover a wide range of approaches which have really only come into prominence in the last twenty years. This approach owes its present strength to a number of factors. Essentially, it is an attempt to come to terms with the whole distressed person, rather than simply with that intellectual part of his mind to which most verbal therapies address themselves. There is, further-more, a refusal to look into the past for causes, but an emphasis upon the 'here and now'. Perls (1973) talks of a concern with the 'what and how' of action rather than the 'why'.

Clients are not usually those who are ill in the traditional psychiatric sense, but rather those people who feel a dis-ease, a distress, and that they are out of touch with the world in which they find themselves. A shorthand for this might be found in the sociological term of *alienation* — an estrange-ment between man and his society. In passing, it is worth recalling that the term 'alienist' was applied to the earliest psychiatrists. Therapy then presents itself as a vehicle not for treatment as such, but for something closer to personal growth. The actual practices may vary, from something akin to group therapy, to psychodrama and to whole—body activities which involve physical activities as well as mental ones. The emphasis throughout is upon present feelings and the clear and unequivocal expression of these to others. Emphasis is placed upon direct expression, both as it applies to the individual talking to another person and as it applies to the individual referring to him- or herself. Interactive games and role-playing may be used to spark off activities, loosen up communication and to facilitate self-learning.

In such circumstances to talk of 'cures' is inappropriate and hence outcome studies are rarely produced. The aim is really closer to an educational model of change than a medical one. The concerns are future-orientated — equipping people to face life more adequately and to cope better with future changes.

Conclusion

In presenting these alternative approaches we have had to be

both cursory and highly selective. Some of the approaches
that we describe may be absorbed very easily into the social
casework mainstream or the eclectic approach that we
advocate, others may be applied on a selective basis. Individual social workers may have to take things into their own
hands if they want to develop their skills in these areas. This
may involve first of all reading; second, seeking out appropriate training courses, third, finding colleagues, either within
social work, or related fields, who already practice these techniques and finally obtaining either formal or informal supervision. These steps may not come easily, in a busy social-
work agency, but they will enable the interested social worker
to continue to develop as a therapist and avoid the stagnation
inherent in routine activities.

6

Social Work and Schizophrenia: a Case Study

Introduction

In this chapter our aim is to present a case as an example in order to illustrate the range of work that a social worker may be called upon to perform with a particular client, in this case, a young man suffering from schizophrenia. The techniques involved are common to social work in many settings and the presence of mental illness is only one facet of a case which might just as well have involved work with someone with a physical handicap or with a young offender about to leave institutional care.

The referral

John was admitted, as a matter of emergency, to a large psychiatric hospital, one Sunday afternoon. The events surrounding the admission seemed a little unclear, but the family practitioner had made the request at the instigation of the boy's family. John had been accompanied to hospital by his father. The admission staff understood that he had just left school and was to enter the RAF on some form of apprenticeship scheme.

Initial contact

Faced, on a Monday morning, with a 16-year-old boy occupying a bed in an otherwise adult ward, the psychiatrist requested that a social worker conduct a home visit as quickly as possible. The boy, John, appeared to be hallucinating; he smiled a good deal for no apparent reason, appeared to be listening to voices, and at times would appear frightened and tearful. A tentative diagnosis of schizophrenia was made, but at this stage a diagnosis of a drug-induced problem was not ruled out.

The social worker's brief was to gather a full social history (see Appendix I), enquire about possible drug abuse, uncover the circumstances that led up to the admission and finally to assess the parents' readiness for John's return home when his symptoms began to subside. A telephone appointment was made to see the parents on the following evening.

The first home visit

The home was a modest semi-detached house, well decorated and maintained, but in an area which was beginning to decline. The social worker was given a chilling welcome, which never warmed throughout the hour or so it was necessary to spend in order to extract the information. Both parents were present and a fleeting appearance was made by John's sister, some two years his junior. This was the only time that Mrs H. unfroze and cast a warm smile in the daughter's direction. John's father, who hovered at the edge of the room, and the conversation, was a librarian. The fact that he was '*only* a librarian', and earned little for a man in his forties was pointed out, on more than one occasion, by his wife.

The picture they (although Mrs H. was the major informat) presented, was one of a boy who had few friends and appeared not to enjoy life very much. He had few outside interests – a vague concern for the local football team seemed the extent of them – and increasingly spent long hours in his room constructing plastic aircraft. 'I won't have them in this room – they attract so much dust,' said Mrs H. sharply – Mr H. responded with a watery smile.

John's remoteness and 'silliness' has increased in recent months, as the end of his school life approached. There had been incidents in which he had climbed out of his bedroom window; attacked a neighbour's small child for no apparent reason, and eventually barricaded himself into his bedroom. A running battle it seems, was conducted between the two siblings, with John the focus of most of the blame.

Both parents had noticed the lengthening periods of preoccupation, which the family doctor had correctly taken to be spells of hallucination. Involvement with drugs did not appear to be likely. The events on Sunday, only days before he was due to enter the RAF., started with a fight with his sister and ended with him in his bedroom threatening to jump out of the window. The doctor who had been called out to deal with similar incidents before, suggested and then arranged a voluntary admission to hospital. Although at first it had been thought that compulsory powers under the Mental Health Act Chapter 10) would be required, in fact John had been talked out of his bedroom, and went willingly, if miserably to hospital.

Major themes to emerge from the interview were the following:

1. John was regarded by his parents as an academic 'failure', unable to live up to the example set by his sister who was intelligent, hard-working, and a talented musician.
2. John was regarded as disruptive to the harmony of the family. His parents repeatedly stressed that he needed containing and that they would not have him back home.
3. A major concern they expressed was how far this 'breakdown' would endanger the chances of John entering the Services, which they seemed to see as the best way of getting him off their hands.

Further family interviews were not wanted, as they made it clear that John was 'ill' and that they wanted him 'sorting out'. Their own possible involvement in the situation was not something that they were prepared to examine.

The worker left feeling frustrated and a little angry.

The first interview with John

John was tearful and confused when the social worker met him for the first time, some three days after admission. He appeared to be still hallucinating as he would break the conversation and 'listen' to voices, becoming absorbed and detached.

The problems faced by John were complex and each contributed to the other. There was a danger that in trying to understand and disentangle them, the social worker might attribute them all to the illness. There was of course the fact that he was displaying many of the symptoms associated with schizophrenia, but a number of other factors coloured this picture:

1. This was the first extended period John had spent away from home.
2. He was ambivalent about his parents, to whom he wanted to return, but from whom he feared rejection.
3. He was also in the middle of a fairly normal adolescent rebellious phase.

All these factors, together with a healthy dislike for the hospital, contributed to his being anxious and tearful, but at the same time aggressive and prepared to kick against the limits imposed upon him.

During this first interview the social worker concentrated upon John's feelings about being away from home for the first time. This was an immediate concern for him and at the same time something which could be discussed on a realistic level. The temptations to explore the pathology or indulge in attempts to uncover potentially powerful family dynamics were resisted.

The school visit

The school was a traditional grammar school, which somewhat reluctantly had 'gone comprehensive'. Both the headmaster and the form master were interviewed. The impression they gave was of a boy who had always had to struggle academically in the school environment. Unfortunately he did not possess any sporting, musical or other talents, which might have made up for his deficiencies. This was in stark contrast to his younger sister who was academically bright, a good athlete and a gifted cellist. She attended the same school and constant reference was made to her. Apparently John's father had previously attended the same school and had been extremely concerned that his son should follow in his footsteps. The headmaster gave the impression that it was this special pleading which had obtained the place for John.

In his early school days John had simply lagged a little behind his peers, but over the previous two to three years had become increasingly disruptive in the classroom. This had taken the form of 'silly' behaviour, hiding people's books and irritating other boys while they tried to work — nothing very serious or malicious, but sufficient for him to have been dubbed a 'pest' about the place. Most recently his behaviour had become, in their terms, 'rather strange'. He had periods of vagueness, when he would sit blank-faced, apparently unaffected by the world around him. He appeared indifferent to any punishments meted out to him and quite unconcerned at his failure, for example, to arrive with any completed homework. 'He didn't feel the need to invent an excuse', said his bemused form master.

The team meeting on the ward had raised the possibility of a return to school for a further year if his symptoms subsided rapidly. This notion was firmly squashed by the teachers, who gave the impression that they were glad to see the back of him.

The social worker was surprised that having observed John's behaviour they had not taken action to refer him to the school psychological service. Their parting comment was to the effect that they were 'shocked, but not surprised' on learning that he had been admitted to a psychiatric hospital.

Life in the hospital

John was by no means a model patient as far as the hospital

was concerned. He quickly became bored on the admission ward and began to annoy many of the other patients, deliberately setting out to provoke them. Part of the reason for this appeared to be the need he felt to demonstrate that he was different from them. During the sessions with the social worker he made repeated references to 'those mad people', and asserted 'I'm not like them'. Many of them were much older and rather ponderous in thought and movement. He exploited this by shifting chairs as they prepared to sit down, tripping them up and so on. Something which may have been seen as high spirits in a schoolroom was however viewed very differently in a hospital. Nursing staff began to press for him to be moved to a more secure ward.

A vicious spiral was beginning to develop, with restrictions leading to 'acting out', followed by further restriction. A half-hearted attempt to 'escape' home one day led to curtailment of privileges, and finally John jumped from a window onto the roof of a consultant's new car. This led to his transfer to another ward.

The range of occupational opportunities open to John around the hospital was fairly limited. Many of them consisted of dull routine assembling or packing jobs. So dull were some of these that it was difficult not to agree with John when he said 'If you're not mad when they send you, you soon will be.' A protracted period of negotiation then began, with the social worker acting as go—between. The consultant, nursing staff, occupational therapy staff and John himself all had to be involved, cajoled and pressured into accepting a formula which would break the cycle of containment and acting out. This involved finding something that John liked doing (working in the printing shop), insisting upon his maintaining regular attendance and agreeing a series of target dates when privileges would be returned and his eventual transfer to a more pleasant and open ward arranged. Setting all this up and supporting John through this period involved a good deal of social—work time and persuasive influence.

Further home visits

Pressure was building up within the hospital for the parents to agree to a regular pattern of weekends at home. The social worker too was being pressurised by the team to arrange this. However, visits to the home were difficult to arrange and less than satisfactory. Appointments were missed, and the parents unbending. An attempt by the consultant, to force their hand, resulted in a distressed John being returned to the hospital one Sunday morning by his father. The parents repeatedly made it clear that it was the hospital's problem and that if John needed nursing staff and a hospital ward during the week he certainly needed them at weekends as well. Mrs H. never visited the hospital during John's stay, although her husband visited him most weeks, without her knowledge.

Further sessions with John

Direct work with John continued, although it was never invasive. The focus was always upon the reality of the situation and immediate short-term goals. Every 'success' in meeting the agreed targets on the work programme was reinforced and rewarded. A student social worker had agreed that when John had completed four weeks uninterrupted work in the print shop he would take him to a floodlit football match. This was done with mutual enjoyment and no incidents.

The following week the ward-transfer was made and discussions began on the possibility of finding a job outside the hospital.

Preparation for job-seeking

John was quite unrealistic about the type of job he wanted or thought he might obtain. He also did not know how to conduct himself in an interview nor the appropriate questions to ask an employer in order to demonstrate an interest in the job on offer.

After discussing the case with a clinical psychologist it was decided to conduct a limited number of social skills training sessions with John, focusing upon the issue of job applications and interviews.

Whilst not unintelligent John failed to concentrate upon

tasks, think about things before he started them or focus upon a single activity at a time. The task in four sessions was to try to enable him to look at these aspects of himself, to identify his own weaknesses, and by role-playing and practice to improve his competence. Use was made of a small portable video-unit to record simulated interviews and to play them back. A bonus to emerge from the sessions was the fact that John said he felt far less nervous about facing an interview — something which formerly he had regarded as very threatening.

Into employment

John was interviewed by the disablement resettlement officer (DRO) who discussed with him the kind of work he would like to do and the possible vacancies open to him. The DRO found him unrealistic in his expectations of the kind of job he could command, and contradictory in his demands — 'outside, but not in the winter'; 'on his own, but with friendly people to work with' — and rather naive in the type of questions he asked. One of John's major concerns, for example, was the number of days leave he would have at Christmas, even though it was then only nearly the end of July.

After discussing the interview with the social worker, and being frankly pessimistic about the possibilities, the DRO agreed to contact an employer close to the hospital who had proved sympathetic in the past. The aim was to find John a job close enough to the hospital for him to use it as a kind of hostel, but at the same time near to his family home so that eventually he could return there and continue with the job.

Work

John managed to attend the job interview on his own, although he grew increasingly anxious as the time for it approached. He returned to the hospital in high excitement to announce that he had been engaged at a local factory at a salary of £10,000 per year! In fact he had been taken on, for a rather humbler wage, to help load delivery trucks. The factory was a lengthy walk away from the hospital, but nonetheless on a direct bus route to his home.

A job outside meant an automatic transfer to a villa in the grounds of the hospital. This was run as a hostel and was intended as a transitional unit between hospital and home. The extra freedom this gave and the fact that for example, meals tended to be prepared individually, was much appreciated by John, for whom the ward and the close proximity to other patients had always proved oppressive.

One of the secondary goals in obtaining employment for John had been to convince his parents that he was now more, reliable and that this in turn would make them more co-operative about weekends. It had been the plan that he should return directly home on a Friday evening from work. The fact of John working at all appeared, in his parents' eyes, to be less important than the fact that it was such a menial task — 'working class and worthless' was their comment.

Social work contact was maintained with John by means of short discussions about his day at work when he returned in the evening. His parents meanwhile refused a request for a further home visit and still resisted attempts on the part of the hospital to extend the period of time John spent at home. This was still confined to late Saturday afternoon departures from the hospital and a return soon after Sunday lunchtime.

Some two weeks after John had started work the social work department was contacted by an irate employer. It appeared that a fight had broken out in the yard, culminating in John throwing stones at some of his workmates, one of whom had sustained 'a broken nose'. When the social worker arrived at the factory it was found that the mayhem created by John was not quite as serious as the urgent telephone call might have suggested. The 'broken nose' turned out to be simply bruised and apart from a few cuts and a bit of blood no serious damage had been done. However, John got his cards.

The story he told was a fairly typical one. His workmates had naturally questioned him about where he lived and what work he had done before. Unable lightly to pass off his hospital address, he had exposed a weakness which they began to exploit. Initially this took the form of sending him on fool's errands — fruitless trips round the factory in search of 'sky-hooks'. Then they began to call him names and mimic his facial grimacing and hesitancy of speech. While he was loading a truck this reached a crescendo of derision and he responded by throwing a box at somebody. A 'playground' battle then commenced which was all too much for the foreman who called in the manager. This simply confirmed John's parents' belief that he was unfit to live at home.

Further pressure was applied by the hospital on his parents to extend the period of time John spent at home. His father responded by taking him to stay for a full weekend with his parents some fifty miles away, with whom John had a good relationship. John returned to work in the occupational therapy unit, but retained his place in the villa. Weekends with grandparents became established as part of the regular pattern, with only occasional returns home.

Future planning

The social work discussions with John focused upon the problems he had encountered at the factory, the need to look for a new job and the ambivalence he felt towards his parents and the visits to his grandparents. It transpired that his grandparents ran a small transport café and that John was being drawn into helping them at weekends. He appeared to enjoy this work and the suggestion was made that he might like to extend his visit to a full week. A visit to the grandparents confirmed that they were willing to have him and that he was indeed an asset to them in the café. He was not the world's best worker, but he seemed cheerful enough most of the time and when he had 'one of his funny moods', he was deputed to work in the kitchens on his own 'out of harm's way'. After some eight weeks, and gradually extending weekends, John was discharged from hospital to his grandparents' home.

The final home visit

A final home visit was arranged in order to return some books found in John's locker and to clear up some administrative details. Almost as a parting comment the social worker said that they would have to drop all idea of John joining the RAF. John's mother turned to her husband and said 'Yes, for the same reasons that you had to leave it'. They then revealed for the first time (in spite of direct questioning during the first interview) that John's father had been invalided out of the RAF when he had had a 'nervous break- down'. A promising career as a pilot officer was cut short and in this wife's eyes her husband had never been able to command a job or a social position like it since. The hostility which had been built up between them then and never expressed, found in John the perfect vehicle for them to fight out this longstanding conflict.

Analysis

A brief analysis of John's situation will facilitate the further understanding of our model of intervention outlined in Chapter 3. John's case history well illustrates the emphasis we placed there upon understanding the individual's unique experience of mental illness and its impact upon him and his family. It also highlights the importance of understanding the difference between the 'form' of the syndrome and the 'content' through which the condition is manifested. Again and again the social worker had to differentiate between what were possibly distortions of ego-functioning with a misinterpretation of reality by John and eliciting the reality of the here-and-now family interaction. It will have been noted that the social worker always respected John's defences and was never invasive. However, when it was appropriate a behaviourally based model was used. This involved working within a time-limited framework in order to examine social skills and improve John's ability to cope with situations such as interviews or jobs.

Conclusion

John's disability remains and may continue for the rest of his life. However, the medication which he takes controls the major symptoms, leaving him as somebody who appears a little bit strange, but who can nonetheless form relationships and continue to work.

Social work intervention involved:

(a)   information gathering
(b)   direct counselling with John and his family
(c)   environmental manipulation
(d)   advocacy
(e)   the use of behavioural techniques
(f)   attempt to integrate and co-ordinate

In such circumstances it may not be realistic to talk about a cure. However, the disorder is now sufficiently contained for him to lead an independent existence and enjoy life, if not to the full, at least to the limits of his handicap.

Theoretical note

It has been thought for a long time that close involvement in family life could increase the likelihood of a further breakdown in somebody diagnosed as suffering from schizophrenia (Brown, 1959). Relapse and further hospital treatment appeared to be more likely for some ex-patients if they were discharged to their parental or marital home, instead of to a hostel, to other relatives or to live on their own.

Brown and his colleagues tried to capture the particular atmosphere present in some families by the concept of *expressed emotion*. By this he meant the number of critical comments relatives made about the patient. High levels of expressed emotion, when measured in a family, proved to be a good predictor of relapse.

Brown took a sample of just over 100 discharged schizophrenic patients and found that within nine months one—third had relapsed (Brown *et al.*, 1972). However, within the group categorised as living in homes where there was high expression of emotion (EE) 58 per cent of ex-patients relapsed, compared with only 16 per cent in homes where there was low expression of emotion. The amount of time a patient and his family spent in face-to-face contact also seemed to be a factor, since those ex-patients with thirty-five hours per week of exposure or more were found to be most at risk. In a further series of studies Vaughn and Leff (1976) found that both medication and 'controlled contact' − for example, encouraging the ex-patient to spend time alone in his room at times of tension − could cut relapse rates.

In John's case the social worker was picking up a great deal of 'expressed emotion' during the home visits. The hospital staff, for the best of motives, were eager for John to return home, and the social worker tried to convey this to the parents. However, all attempts to persuade the family simply resulted in a flare-up of symptoms for John.

The grandparents provided the ideal solution. They were more tolerant of John's behaviour, perhaps because they were less directly involved in it. But at the same time they could offer a task which provided John with some stimulation and which, furthermore, he enjoyed doing. At times of tension his retreat into the kitchen of the café, or to his own room acted as sufficient safety valve for him to contain his problems and remain outside hospital.

7

Drugs and Physical Treatment

Drugs and the social worker

Many social workers remain sceptical about the use of physical treatment of all kinds in psychiatry. Certainly history is on their side, since some practices, long held to be efficacious, have been abandoned as ineffective. However, regardless of one's personal stance and beliefs the reality is that most people who suffer from psychiatric disorder in this country are going to be treated with some form of physical procedure, most usually drugs. It is important therefore for the social worker to gain some working knowledge of what these treatments entail, how they affect the client, what may be some of the likely side-effects, and how they are likely to affect the relationship between the client, the worker and his family.

There are, we think, very real grounds why social workers should examine the role of drugs in their relationship with their clients, setting aside the issue of how much good they do to the individual, or how helpful they are in controlling disturbing and disruptive feelings and symptoms.

The dangers of addiction

Social workers should be alert to the fact that some drugs (anxiolytics/and hypnotics) used in psychiatry may lead to addiction, or, at the very least, dependence. If the workers suspect that this is happening they should attempt to bring it to the notice of both client and doctor.

Overdoses

Most drugs, including those used in psychiatry, are dangerous in overdose. Social workers deal with a clientele which is subject to suicidal attempts and gestures, most usually by means of drug overdoses. These two facts should always be borne in mind in one's work with clients. If the worker senses that the client is becoming suicidal this should be brought to the notice of anybody prescribing the drugs.

Side-effects

Any drug which is powerful enough to be of any use is also going to produce side-effects. In prescribing drugs doctors should always be aware of this and weigh up the balance of advantage. For the social worker a knowledge of side-effects is important for two reasons. First, if spotted, it may be necessary to communicate the fact to the medical team. Second, it may be necessary to offer reassurance to both client and his family about the side-effects. This may mean encouraging somebody to continue taking medication in the knowledge that the side-effects will subside or that symptoms will appear. Encouragement may also be necessary when it is known that a drug takes some time to achieve any therapeutic effect.

The social work relationship

It is important to know if a client is taking drugs so that any impact these may have upon the client's ability to make a relationship is understood. They may, for example, make the client feel drowsy during the early days of treatment.

Employment

A knowledge of medication may be necessary in discussing

the client's potential for work. Some types of jobs may prove unsuitable, for example, to people on certain kinds of medication. Temporary difficulties may occur when the dosage is being increased. In such cases time off may have to be negotiated.

Medication and social work goals

The drugs being taken by a client may undermine the wider treatment programme. For example, if the social worker's goal is to help an individual face up to a certain problem or overcome a particular anxiety, then the individual's resolve may be weakened by the belief that 'a pill will take away the problem'. Similarly, any behaviourally based programme may be seriously disrupted, and consistency lost, if medication is altered during its course. Such potential clashes of therapeutic intent may only be resolved by discussion, teamwork and compromise.

Psychological impact

Drugs act upon the individual on a number of levels, not least of which is the psychological. All types of medicine are invested with a variety of symbolic meanings. To the individual they may indicate that his symptoms have been taken seriously; that he is genuinely ill, that modern scientific knowledge is being applied to his problem and that the solution to his difficulty is now out of his hands.

In such circumstances a social work intervention may appear rather humdrum or unnecessary. The social worker too may react to the medication. He may resent the apparent power invested in it by his client, and feel that his own contribution is undervalued.

Drugs

There seem to be two opposing views about the use of

psychotropic drugs those used for the treatment of psychiatric illness) held by the general public — and presumably shared by social workers. There are those who, apparently increasingly, look to their doctor, and the medicine cupboard, for the relief of all kinds of distress. Everyday misery, family crises and problems in sleeping are increasingly being seen as appropriate forms of 'disease' for powerful pharmacological treatment. Some have tried to blame the family practitioner for this apparent over-recourse to drug treatments, pointing to heavy caseloads and a paucity of training in counselling skills as mitigating factors. However, part of the problem lies with the patient, who frequently expects and even demands a prescription at the end of a consultation, almost as a symbol of the reality of his problem. Professor Trethowan (1975) has pointed out that about a quarter of all drug-prescription is now for some form of psychiatric disorder, and has questioned the whole, 'pills for personal problems' approach.

On the other hand, there are those people who remain very suspicious of medication, particularly when it is intended to affect mood or behaviour. They tend to point to harmful side-effects, habituation and addiction, and question the way in which pain and anxiety, which might otherwise be purposive, is simply blotted out. Both points of view are in some part correct. We do, as a society, reach too easily for the medicine bottle (or the whisky bottle!) when confronted by discomfort; doctors are overworked and ill-prepared for patients with personal problems. All drugs are likely to result in side-effects for some people and a few may lead to dependence and addiction. However, when used with discretion there is no doubt that modern psychotropic drugs have relieved a great deal of pain and distress — not only for the patients, but also for their families.

The aim of this section will be to introduce the main types of psychotropic drugs currently in use, to mention some of their likely side-effects and to point to the implications for the social worker when a client is taking such forms of medication. One of the difficulties in talking about drugs is that many appear under a number of different names. Each has an approved pharmacological name, but each manufacturer produces his own version which is given a trade name. The drug's industry is fiercely competitive and companies constantly battle to produce new products, or at least variations upon established ones, in order to claim a share of the market. In Appendix II we list the preparations in most common use under both pharmacological and trade names.

Anti-psychotic or major tranquillisers

By far the most important drug in this group of drugs − those largely concerned with controlling the symptoms of schizophrenia − is chlorpromazine. The importance of this drug, which with others of the phenothiazine group, has in many people's eyes revolutionised psychiatric practices, lies in its ability to control certain symptoms without reducing the patient to a state of stupor. Restless and hallucinated patients formerly had to be contained either by physical means or by the use of medication such as paraldehyde which used to cloud consciousness, induce sleep and was addictive. Modern major tranquillisers, when properly used, have facilitated the return to the community of many formerly hospitalised patients, and enabled them to resume jobs and continue a reasonably normal family life. It is important to remember that such medication does not 'treat' the disorder but does effectively suppress the symptoms. The individual is enabled to appear less abnormal by suppressing his symptoms of hallucinations, irritability, restlessness and thought disorder. Relapse rates have also been affected by this form of help.

Drugs manufacturers continue to produce a number of variations on the major tranquilliser theme, claiming that each has a slightly different effect or produces fewer side-effects. The evidence from drug trials indicates that they are all fairly similar in effectiveness. However, individuals do vary in sensitivity to side-effects and this may prompt the clinician to change the medication.

For the social worker and the family the major problems may be created by the variety of side-effects that the major tranquillisers are likely to produce in the client. One of the most problematic of these for the patient is that the drug may leave him feeling sleepy in the early stages of treatment. The other side-effects can be more bizarre and particularly distressing to the family. The symptoms produced may be categorised into four types:

(1) Parkinsonism, in which the symptoms produced are identical to those found in the disorder which bears that name. It is characterised by a tremor, sometimes described as 'pill rolling' in that the client will move thumb and forefinger as if rolling a small ball between them. He may be somewhat rigid in stance and walk in a shuffling kind of way, with arms still and unswinging by his side. The rigidity may extend to the face, producing a mask-like appearance, with associated difficulties in swallowing and occasional dribbling of saliva.

(2) Dystonic crisis. This is of more sudden onset and consists of muscular spasms usually of the mouth, tongue and jaw. A condition known as the oculogyric crisis may also occur. Typically, the patient at first adopts a fixed stare, then their eyes move to one side to be followed by a backward tilting of the head. Both this side-effect and Parkinsonism are usually successfully controlled by anti-Parkinsonian drugs which are often given in tandem with major tranquillisers (Benzhexol [Artane], Benztropine [Cogentin], Orphenadrine [Disipal], Procyclidine [Kemadrin]).

(3) Akathisia may develop after taking the medication for some days. This means literally, an inability to sit down, but is more typically just jittery, restless behaviour.

(4) Tardive dyskinesia which is quite rare may develop. This only becomes apparent after some years of treatment. It develops gradually, is usually confined to the elderly and is usually irreversible. The patient may develop a facial grimace, make chewing movements, grunt and, once again, appear fidgety.

With these potential side-effects (fortunately not common)

it is not surprising that both client and family may find the medication undesirable. This is a particular problem when, as may be the case, the client or patient is urged to continue the medication long after the initial psychotic symptoms have disappeared to prevent relapse. The social worker in such cases has an obligation not only to work with client and family but also to keep open the channels of communication with the medical team. It may be that a lower dosage, change of medication, or increase in anti-Parkinsonian drug may provide the answer. A simple explanation to both client and family may also help to contain the situation.

As already indicated, it is often necessary to continue medication for some time. This fact, together with the difficulties experienced in getting clients to take medication regularly, has led the drug manufacturers to produce a range of so-called 'depot' preparations. These are becoming an increasingly popular way of maintaining psychotic patients outside hospital with the assurance that medication is being maintained. The injection contains the active agent in a suspension of an oil-like substance. This ensures the gradual release of the drug into the bloodstream over a period of two to four weeks. Patients are requested to attend regular clinics at the hospital or are visited by community psychiatric nurses. There is now good evidence that this prevents relapse in many cases, and reduces the need for readmission to hospital.

Anti-depressants

The term antidepressant may be a little misleading since by elevating mood these drugs are essentially concerned with improving the *symptoms* of the depressed phase of affective disorders. These symptoms include those usually associated with depression, namely loss of appetite, insomnia, lack of energy, loss of interest, etc., but also anxiety and irritability towards others,. There is some evidence that the irritability associated with depression may be related to incidents of non-accidental injury to young children. One complication of this is that doctors have been in the habit of prescribing drugs of the benzodiazepine group (diazepam, nitrazepam) to women in order to help them to sleep when they complained of mild depressive symptoms. It seems likely that one of the side-effects, in some people, is increased irritability, thus compounding the problems and potentially increasing the risks of child-abuse.

The most commonly used group of drugs to combat depression are the tricyclics estimated to be effective in about 60 per cent of cases. They may be found in many guises and under various trade names. Their effectiveness appears to be similar in most cases, the major variations being found in individual responses particularly with regard to side-effects. The following listing is not exhaustive:

Approved name	*Commercial name*
Amitriptyline	Tryptizol, Lentizol, Saroten
Nortriptyline	Aventyl, Allegron
Imipramine	Tofranil, Norpramine
Clomipramine	Anafranil

This group of drugs has two major disadvantages. The first is that they are slow to act – taking from one to three weeks in order to become effective. The second is that, particularly early on, they may produce the following side-effects: drowsiness, dry mouth, headaches and difficulty in passing urine, the last applying particularly to the elderly. With initial side-effects, and no positive improvement, compliance is often a difficulty. The further disadvantage is that in the case of somebody severely depressed, who may be suicidal, the delay in a drug taking effect may prove fatal. In such cases immediate resort to ECT (electro convulsant therapy) is frequently made.

For the social worker then, a client taking such medication presents a number of problems. First, the fact that the individual may be rather drowsy in interviews. Second, there is the question of compliance and the social worker may need to be quite persuasive if the client is not simply going to throw the whole lot away. Finally, there is always the risk of a dangerous overdose. Here the social worker should be aware of possible hoarding and perhaps even involve other members of the family in trying to keep an eye on the situation. This may prove difficult and obviously requires a good deal of tact on the part of the social worker, but it may be necessary if a tragedy is to be avoided.

If tricyclics prove unsuccessful the drugs of the monoamine oxidase inhibitors group (MAOI) may be tried. Some of the commonest are Phenelzine (Nardil), Isocarboxazid (Marplan) and Tranylcypromine (Parnate). They used to be more widely used but are now used by most clinicians only for atypical depressions. In effect they appear unpredictable, and patients have to follow a prescribed dietary regime, avoiding amine-rich foods (cheese, broad beans, Oxo) with moderation in alcoholic intake. Failure to do so will result in raised blood pressure and severe headaches. Patients on such drugs should carry a warning card, avoid any anaesthetics (for example at the dentist) and be careful about taking other medication in combination with the antidepressant.

Lithium

Lithium carbonate is now commonly precribed for patients suffering from mania, recurrent depressive illness or manic-depressive illness. Lithium is taken, not when an attack occurs, but all the time as a prophylaxis (that is, a preventative) against an outbreak of the illness. Normally side-effects should not occur since a patient ought to be attending a clinic regularly in order to have his blood level checked. In properly controlled doses Lithium is very effective, safe and does not result in any side-effects which could affect the social work relationship. However, the difference between a therapeutic dose and a dangerous one is small, and there remain doubts about possible long-term kidney damage.

Hypnotics

Hypnotics are drugs which induce sleep. Many psychiatrically-ill patients, particularly those who are depressed or anxious, experience difficulties in both getting to sleep and staying asleep. As Trethowan (1975) notes, 40 per cent of the psychoactive drugs prescribed are some form of hypnotic, indicating something of the size of the problem, particularly in general practice. Drugs of the barbiturate group have traditionally been used in this role, but their use is declining. It is now clear that they do become addictive, disturb normal sleep patterns and may be used in overdose for suicide attempts. Much more common are drugs of the benzodiazepine group. Diazepam and nitrazepam are two which are frequently prescribed and both are relatively safe in overdose, but, as we indicated earlier, they too have drawbacks.

Minor tranquillisers

As their name suggests these drugs are used to relieve tension and anxiety mainly in people suffering from neurotic disorders of various kinds. The readiness with which doctors, mainly family practitioners, prescribe such drugs as librium and valium, particularly to women who seem to be responding to external stresses of various kinds, has come in for much criticism. Most drugs of this type produce drowsiness in some people and may cause ataxia -- a disturbance in the co-ordination of voluntary movements especially in older people. Social workers frequently work with people under the influence of these drugs, sometimes without realising it. The clients may appear sluggish and unresponsive, and complain of feeling tired. This may create particular problems for the family or for an employer.

Electro-convulsive therapy

The use of electro convulsive therapy (ECT) is something about which many social workers feel strongly. They point to the apparently barbaric practice of passing electricity through the brain in order to induce a convulsion. They question the fact that there is little knowledge of how the shock is supposed to affect the individual, or whether it will cause him distress. Finally, they express concern about potential damage to the patient particularly with regard to loss of memory. In each of these instances there are valid points, but what is often neglected is the fact that ECT is really our most effective weapon against certain kinds of life—threatening depressive disorders, with about 72 per cent of those who are treated this way receiving profound relief.

The modern application of ECT is not such a terrifying experience and any social worker dealing with people who receive it, should ask to be allowed to observe the process. The procedure is as follows: patients are prepared as if for an operation, since they will be rendered unconscious by an anaesthetic. This means that they are not given anything to eat or drink for at least four hours before the session — something worth remembering if you have clients attending for ECT as out-patients. About one or two hours before the treatment the patient may be given a tranquilliser if he appears anxious. The patient is usually wheeled into the treatment room from the waiting area on a mobile trolley. A drug called atropine is then given. This is quite usual before anaesthesia and serves to dry up saliva and bronchial secretions. A quick-acting anaesthetic, usually thiopentone, is then administered together with a muscle-relaxant. Unconsciousness is followed by paralysis, so that the patient remains unaware of this process. Oxygenation becomes necessary as the paralysis extends to the chest, inhibiting lung-function and breathing. The electric shock is then administered via two electrodes placed to the head. This may be either side of the temples, (*bilateral ECT*) but many psychiatrists now favour *unilateral ECT* where both electrodes are placed on only one side of the head, dependant upon the dominant hemisphere. It is believed by some authorities that this reduces the possibility of memory disturbance and confusion. The shock induces an epileptic-like fit, but because of the paralysis this only registers as a trembling of the toes. The procedures take only a couple of minutes from start to finish and the patient is wheeled out to a recovery room and continues to receive oxygen until the effects of the muscle-relaxant wear off. The patient often experiences a headache upon regaining consciousness and may be a little confused for up to an hour. Social work intervention should be avoided on any day in which ECT is to be given.

A good deal of debate surrounds the issue of memory-loss occasioned by ECT. The evidence is rather contradictory and is compounded by the fact that depression itself may cause disturbances of memory. Interestingly enough it is not something of which patients themselves complain; they appear to be more concerned about the privacy and conditions under which treatment is given. There was a vogue for administering ECT on the hospital ward, rather than in a separate treatment unit and this could well be unsettling to other patients. Most hospitals now have a special unit.

The other point made by critics of ECT is that it is potentially dangerous. However, the figures indicate that it is no more dangerous than receiving any form of anaesthetic, for example, from the dentist. Deaths do occur as a result of anaesthesia and figures in the order of 4 to 9 per 100,000 treatments of ECT have been collected. However, one must set alongside these figures those of suicides amongst severely depressed people. It has been estimated that, if left untreated, 11 per cent of those so depressed as to warrant ECT would kill themselves over a period of five years.

For severely depressed patients, particularly those who are suicidal, ECT may still be the best form of treatment available. At the moment a number of *double-blind studies* (i.e. both patient and doctor being unaware of the form of treatment, if any, which has been given) are being conducted and we may have to wait until the results of these are published before the debate can be taken any further.

Psycho-surgery

The whole notion of operating on the brain, or psychosurgery, is a highly emotive one. Nowadays, it is a fairly rare practice, and one confined to those unfortunate people with intractable psychiatric conditions which refuse to yield to any other form of treatment. Usually an individual concerned has spent years in tormented agitation or depression before the decision to operate is taken. Results tend to be blurred by the rhetoric of those who support such operative techniques and those who oppose it. Few clinically-based trials have ever been conducted so that the field is left open for zealots of either group to proclaim their views. The actual surgical practices have improved in recent years and the impact on the brain is now much more conservative. However, when planning to change an organ as delicate as the brain, in an irreversible way, great caution is surely necessary. The present campaigns against psychosurgery may at least result in the whole issue being brought into wider and more open discussion.

The implications for social workers are far-reaching. Any suggestion of such an operation will undoubtedly arouse a great deal of distress and anxiety in the client's family and much of this may be felt by the social worker concerned. In such circumstances the social worker should establish that every other course of action has been considered and that, in Clare's terms (Clare, 1976), 'the price to be paid for symptomatic relief' is not too great. Finally, should the operation be carried out, there will follow the need for an intensive and extensive programme of rehabilitation, in order to help the individual concerned return to the community.

Conclusion

The issue of physical treatments is a complicated one which many social workers view with concern. However, criticisms should not come from a state of ignorance; a working knowledge of the various drugs involved, their likely side-effects, and possible impact upon individual and family is essential if a dialogue is to be established with the medical team. The forum for this debate should be within the multi-disciplinary team preferably at ward level when decisions are being taken. What is emerging, in the light of recent research, is that physical treatments may be more effective if they are placed within the context of other forms of helping. An informed dialogue between the social worker and the doctor will result in a better service for the client and ultimately a greater understanding of psychiatric disorder and its alleviation.

8

Psychiatric Emergencies

By dictionary definition, an emergency is any sudden state of affairs which demands immediate action. In psychiatric terms there are at least three ways of looking at such an event:

(1) the medical viewpoint. Doctors and hospitals are used to coping with physical emergencies in the course of their daily work. Therefore, when some abnormal mental state is the cause of the emergency the remedy is most frequently seen in terms of some form of medical intervention, usually implying the administration of drugs.

(2) the psychological viewpoint. This is less concerned to classify overt symptoms and more willing to see the person in distress as somehow failing to cope with some stressful situation. This failure to cope may be due to the sheer size and impact of the stress or indicative of some breakdown of the usual defensive mechanisms, either because the ego is under-developed and therefore vulnerable, or because it has been undermined by illness.

(3) the social worker's viewpoint. An emergency may be seen as being concerned less with the disturbance within one individual than with a breakdown within a system or a wider group. In these terms the focus shifts from a concern with one person and moves to a consideration of that person within the context of friends, neighbours and relatives.

The emergency may be seen as fulfilling a function for this

wider group, and the social worker intervening should be concerned to ask himself the following questions:

(a)   why has the emergency occurred now?
(b)   what events have preceded it?
(c)   who drew attention to the emergency?
(d)   who are the other people involved in this crisis?
(e)   what part have they played in the build up and outburst?

If the situation is analysed in this way it sometimes emerges that it is another member of the social network who is really the person in crisis and that the apparent victim has been manipulated to take the part of the person with the major problems. It is interesting to discover how often so-called emergencies have in fact been simmering for some time and what has finally sparked it off and led to the call for intervention.

There are at least two reasons why it is important to try to take in this broad picture, rather than simply respond to one individual. First, even if the only immediate recourse is to remove that person from that setting, either for his own safety or that of others, his return and the social worker's subsequent work with both the individual and the wider group will be made easier if an appreciation of the situation at the time of the crisis has been acquired. Once the person presenting the problem has left the situation it may be extremely difficult to open up any discussion and examination of the events that led up to the crisis and hence the worker's attempts to mediate or ameliorate may be hindered. It may be in the interests of those who remain behind to suggest that all is now well and that no help is required. Should the emergency have resulted in a removal to hospital, this attitude may make it difficult to return the individual concerned. This should be an important consideration when trying to decide what action to take. The options include offering, or insisting upon, hospital admission or attempting to resolve the crisis within the home.

Second, appreciation of the individual's behaviour and its relationship to the setting in which it takes place, may be necessary in order to separate a genuine psychiatric emergency from something which may be no less violent or urgent but which does not really have any *psychiatric* component. We live in an age in which we increasingly seek to ascribe any form of violent, deviant or otherwise disturbing behaviour to some psychiatric cause. Some people have seen in this an attempt by medicine to 'colonise' more areas of social life. However, it seems just as likely that, as a society, we wish to invoke the medical model to solve or palliate many of our own problems. The reasons for this are complex but involve some at least of the following factors:

(a) the loss of traditional ways of handling and coping with strongly expressed emotions.
(b) the increased importance we attach to normality
(c) the expansion of the welfare state and the expectations that this arouses
(d) the growth in the number of mental health professionals
(e) the development of a drugs industry which has led to overprescribing
(f) increasing reliance upon pharmacological products.

These factors, following in the wake of industrialisation and the development of scientific medicine, have left people less able and willing to cope with domestic turmoil and more prepared to call upon outsiders for help. Faced with an apparent emergency, say within a family situation, the social worker may find a medical diagnosis being pressed upon him -- 'he's mad', 'he just went berserk', 'he's crazy, he just started throwing things about' are just some of explanations the worker is offered and such lay diagnoses may be difficult to resist! How then is the social worker, on moving into such a fraught and emotionally charged situation, to disentangle the truly medical from the social? How, in other words, is the social worker to decide if what he is seeing is the manifestation of some form of psychiatric disturbance or the result of social pressure and psychological stress? Can he cope with the confusion on his own, or should he contact a doctor, a policeman, or both? These are hypothetical questions which may in practice be unanswerable or at least oversimplistic. What may in reality confront the worker is a dangerous cocktail of all three factors, the psychiatric, the psychological and the social. Psychiatric emergencies are likely to come in a number of guises. The following listing presents in a fairly simple form some of the most common.

Severe depression

The most likely form of presentation in such cases is the threat of suicide which is dealt with elsewhere in this book (see Chapter 9). However, the depressed person may be in danger because of a prolonged refusal to eat or drink in which case admission to hospital may be necessary. Because of the stubbornness with which these two necessities of life have been resisted it is unlikely that a person in such a situation would enter hospital willingly and compulsion may be necessary. In some elderly people a situation akin to 'suicide by neglect' may exist, the will to live having gone and the wish to die having taken over.

Hypomania

The presentation of somebody suffering from hypomania is likely to be the very opposite of somebody with depression. The person suffering from hypomania may exhibit elation, a general speeding up of physical activity and the belief that the world has never been better. He usually manages to keep up this level of frenetic activity with very little sleep and may be uninhibited in his behaviour (in extreme cases the term *hypermania* is applied). For the family such behaviour can be devastating, for they have to put up with not only the amount of physical energy with which the person confronts the world but also a range of behaviour that is sometimes both disruptive and damaging. In this uninhibited state the individual is quite capable of spending all the household money or ordering goods and undertaking hefty HP commitments.

Typically, the individual concerned shows little insight into the condition and may dismiss the suggestion of illness or hospital treatment, understandably, when he feels so well. Nevertheless, admission for a short period of time may be necessary for his own safety.

In some instances the syndromes of *severe depression* and *hypomania* may be associated, the individual swinging from one state to the other.

Schizophrenic disorders

It is likely that in these cases the 'emergency' is of the kind which has been smouldering for some time — the question must always be asked 'why is it an emergency now?' Clearly somebody suffering from the variety of symptoms implied by this term is likely to create a good deal of tension and distress among those with whom he lives. At any time these tensions can erupt and, for whatever reason, something which has been contained suddenly becomes unbearable. However, there are a few special instances in which a crisis might develop suddenly because of some change in the condition.

Catatonia, for example, may result in bouts of intense excitement alternating with periods of stuporous behaviour. Such attacks of excitement are marked by their intensity and the impulsiveness with which the individual is likely to act. Paranoid schizophrenia may also trigger an emergency. Here the most likely cause is the increase in feelings that he is being persecuted. The level of fear invoked may lead to panic attacks and irrational behaviour. It is during the acute episodes of this disorder that potentially dangerous behaviour may occur.

Anxiety states

An anxiety or panic attack may foment an emergency since the symptoms can be extremely alarming not only to the individual concerned but also to those people around him. It is characterised not simply by feelings of intense terror but also a full range of changes in body-functioning such as are normally found when anxiety is experienced:

(a)   Sweating
(b)   palpitations

(c)   tightness in the chest
(d)   a dry mouth.

In the absence of any obvious causal factor — a road accident for example — it is best to consider such attacks as psychiatric and treat them accordingly.

Alcohol and drug withdrawal

The withdrawal of drugs upon which the individual has developed a biological dependency is likely to result in a variety of confusional states which may require rapid medical intervention. Typically, the withdrawal of alcohol from somebody who is habituated results in nausea, sweating, tremors and sickness. Later, the subject may appear confused, mildly hallucinated and even suffer from epileptic fits. Barbiturate withdrawal is similar to that from alcohol but withdrawal from the opiate drugs (heroin, etc.) is quite distinctive. The subject typically feels ill, may appear tearful and suffers from dilation of the pupils and sweating attacks. As the symptoms develop they begin to resemble a flu-like illness with vomiting, diarrhoea and stomach pains. The patient is likely to feel uncomfortable and appear restless and disturbed.

Hysteria

Hysteria is a term which is perhaps too widely used, and has come to mean overexcited and tearful emotionality. The popular press likes to ascribe the behaviour of young fans at rock concerts to this syndrome. Such problems are hardly likely to concern the average social worker — unless he has to deal with it in his own children! However, more strictly used, it applies to somebody who is in such a state as to appear bewildered and unable to remember who he is or where he has been. As described it can be confused with various organically based disorders and care should be taken either to exclude these or, at least, bear the possibility in mind. Typically, this type of disorder is seen as existing for some psychological reason, usually associated with some gain to the individual concerned. However, it must be admitted that in such cases the gain is not always easy to discern and such conditions sometimes remain a mystery. Usually, the immediate problem is tackled with drugs but the underlying difficulties and problems may prove intractable even after psychotherapy. Individuals shy away from any attempt to establish underlying causes and may bring about a series of crises or emergencies which can be trying to anybody, family or professional, who seek to help.

Violence and mental illness

Those who are mentally ill are often associated with violent and aggressive behaviour. This may be because many psychiatric conditions make the individual's behaviour strange, unpredictable, and difficult to interpret. However, the evidence for their being any more dangerous than the rest of the population is slight. Most recently Prins (1980) has thoroughly reviewed the relationship between mental illness and lawbreaking and provides a prescription for dealing with dangerous and potentially dangerous clients. This section draws upon his work to a great extent. He points out that people who choose to be social workers, unlike policemen, do not necessarily have the equipment in terms of training, physique or attitude to deal with violent people. Of necessity, most of them only have to offer a set of social skills to the situation rather than the desire or ability to impose their will by force. However, this presents them with certain advantages since they do not by their presence immediately pose any physical threat to the person we may be seeking to help.

For Prins (1980) there are seven attributes which are necessary in working with a client in a situation of some danger:

(1) Honesty with oneself and an acknowledgement of one's own violent potential. This understanding can only come about through effective support

and supervision from more experienced colleagues.
The colleagues can also alert social workers to their
'blind-spots' and to the dangers of overidentification
and denial.

(2)   Social workers should remember also that a 'panic—
reaction' on their part in a moment of particular
stress may prevent them from hearing significant
words or messages from the client or may blind them
to the importance of certain things that are left
unsaid.

(3)   Social workers need to develop a capacity to take a
rounded and objective view of the person adjudged
to be dangerous or potentially dangerous. This will
include the need for a careful in-depth examination
of the person's social situation and the forces creating
stress — both past and present.

(4)   Trying to present oneself as a 'still centre' in dangerous or potentially dangerous situations. This will
often convey calm to the client. A calm voice, an
averted gaze, and slow calm movements augur for a
better response that a panic-stricken grab (e.g. for
a weapon) or a strident command. Sitting is usually
better than standing since it appears less threatening.

(5)   Being prepared to respond speedily to a developing
crisis — some areas of the country are developing
crisis-intervention teams which are able to provide
temporary 'asylum' should this be needed.

(6)   Sometimes it may be possible to 'talk through' a
potentially dangerous episode. One may be able
to point out likely consequences of actions to those
who are in touch with reality. Information may be
gained from the client which may be of use, for
example details of drug-taking or alcohol abuse.
Similarly, a discussion about the cause of fears or the
individual's intentions may prove helpful.

(7)   Many dangerous clients give some advance warning of
the harm they intend to do to either themselves or
others. Social workers should always be aware of
these, attempt to explore them fully in interviews
and if appropriate try to act on them in advance. For

example, many people faced with such thoughts would appreciate being offered a containing enviroment so that they may be helped and removed from the temptation to act out their ideas and fantasies.

Crisis theory and intervention

It would be wrong to see crisis in only negative terms. Such events clearly present social workers, as helpers, with problems but they also provide them with opportunities for effective intervention. This more optimistic, and purposive, view of crisis is expounded by Gerald Caplan (1964) and his colleagues at Harvard:

For Caplan:

> A crisis is provoked when an individual faced with an obstacle to important life goals finds that it is for the time being insurmountable through the utilization of customary methods of problem solving.

He believes that over time people develop a set of routine problem-solving skills. However, in a totally new situation, or one which impinges upon people very powerfully, these may prove inadequate or inappropriate. At first, as events develop, the individual will feel under stress and experience some discomfort. As the pressures increase so does the tension and mild disorganisation may follow. As the usual methods are tried and fail, anxiety will increase, to be followed by a sense of failure and even guilt. A feeling of helplessness then follows: this may be vented on other people or turned inwards as self-destructive behaviour — self-injury, excessive drinking, etc.

If left in the situation the individual may adopt what Caplan would regard as a maladaptive solution. This might involve running away from the crisis, attempting to repress the emotions evoked, or striking out angrily against it. If no resolution emerges then, in the view of Lindemann (1944), a major disorganisation may follow with a psychotic-like episode ensuing.

If an intervention can be made at an earlier stage of the crisis, before it overwhelms the individual, it presents an opportunity for maturation and change. The individual is said to be in a state of 'flux', and may exhibit signs of increased dependency, a need to ventilate experiences and an openness to suggestion. The need for dependency and the suggestibility may, in Caplan's view, be used by a therapist to help the individual to learn a new set of coping skills, which may be utilised in the absence of crisis in the future.

An interventive model, for use during a crisis, was developed by Caplan and his team. A summary is presented below:

1. Early and frequent support is required. This must be given at the time of the crisis, when the potential for change is at its height, rather than after the crisis has subsided.
2. Dependency needs must be recognised and even encouraged. This may be something that the social worker finds difficult to accept and hard to manage.
3. The social worker, in encouraging dependency, may have to help his client overcome fears that the need for help and assistance indicates weakness.
4. Contacts may have to be kept short but they should be very frequent. In many cases the client should have unlimited access to the worker.
5. The social worker should seek to keep all conversations based upon the reality of the situation and avoid attempts by the client to use defences such as denial or evasion. The client must be confronted with the problem and discouraged from looking for people to blame — either self or others.
6. As well as focusing upon the reality of the situation, the social worker should also be helping his client to move towards positive solutions. The worker must beware of attempts to make him collude in solutions which will prove to be maladaptive.
7. The family and the wider social group should be involved, and the client encouraged not to retreat from the situation.
8. In order to avoid heavy medication being given to the

client — a temptation for any hard-pressed doctor involved — attempts must be made to explain the techniques being used to the clinician, and gather his support.

9. No attempt need be made to seek explanations for the crisis nor lengthy analysis of the reasons why coping skills have broken down or proved maladaptive. The focus should be upon the present, and positive solutions.

In order for such techniques to be used effectively a properly constituted crisis team needs to be developed. Such methods, for example, as open access, do not fit comfortably into normal social services organisational patterns. There is now good evidence from the United States, where crisis teams are widely used, that the need for hospital admission can be reduced and the individual helped to recover and develop. The specially trained teams, sometimes incorporating medical staff, are prepared to spend many hours in a client's home during the crisis period, working with both the person in distress and his family.

This type of endeavour contrasts with our own system whereby the only resource usually available to a social worker or doctor is a psychiatric hospital bed. This may well involve moving the client miles away from the scene of the crisis and making use of the compulsory powers contained within the Mental Health Act. We discuss the use of compulsory powers in Chapter 10.

9

Social Work and Suicide

Introduction

About 3,000 people take their own lives in England and
Wales every year. Far more widespread is the phenomenon
of attempted suicide. Incidence rates are always likely to be
incomplete and at best may be viewed as estimates, but
figures in the order of an annual rate of 200:10,000 for men
aged over 15 and 300:10,000 for women over 15 years of age
are widely quoted.

A good deal of discussion has centred on the subject of
motivation, that is, how many of those people who attempt
suicide seriously intend to kill themselves. It is clear from
talking to people who have taken an overdose of drugs that
their motives may involve an attempt to shock, anger or
produce guilt in the people around them. The motivation
may have been to draw attention to their particular plight
in the hopes of receiving help, attention, or change in those
who surround them. This has led the coining of the term
'parasuicide' (Kreitman, 1977) to indicate behaviour
analogous to suicide, but lacking the intent.

It is perhaps best to envisage suicidal behaviour as existing
along some kind of continuum. At one extreme are those
people who successfully kill themselves and do so after a
good deal of thought and preparation. At the other end of
the continuum may be placed those people who perhaps take
a small overdose, knowing that it will not prove fatal and that
they will soon be discovered. In the middle of this continuum
are those people for whom a suicide attempt represents

playing with the fates, a kind of 'Russian roulette', their survival being placed in the hands of luck or chance. The picture is further confused by the fact that intention may not be truly reflected by events. For example, a relatively small overdose may prove fatal in some cases, so widely varied is the tolerance and reaction to drugs. Similarly discovery may be delayed by some chance event — a husband failing to come home at his usual time, because the car breaks down, or a friend failing to arrive at an appointed time.

Suicide and the social worker

For the social worker, suicidal behaviour poses problems at a number of different levels. First is the trauma experienced by a social worker should a client kill, or attempt to kill, himself. The shock of such an event can set off a whole series of emotional reactions within the worker concerned. It may spark off strong feelings of guilt and doubt about professional competence. The worker may well begin to question what part, if any, he played in the event, what, if anything, he could have done to prevent it. Containing and dealing with such emotionally taxing questions is in a sense part of the job, but it can take its toll. Colleagues, both formally in supervision sessions, and informally, play an important part in helping the social worker concerned to reflect upon their own involvement in the event and, in so far as it is possible, to come to terms with it.

Second is the anxiety provoked by a client whom one considers to be a suicide risk. Appreciating and anticipating the potential for suicidal behaviour in a client is an important part of the social work task. Next comes professional concern about how far the social worker should intervene with clients who are believed to be suicidal. Questions such as 'what, if anything can I do?' or 'what right have I to do anything?' are likely to be uppermost in the worker's mind. Finally, he has to consider what response he, as a social worker, should make to the relatives of those people who have taken or attempted to take their own life.

In the remainder of this chapter we will aim to provide

some information which may be of use to social workers faced by these problems. We begin by trying to round out the picture with regard to suicidal behaviour; where it happens, how and to some extent, why. We then discuss some of the factors associated with suicide and attempt to indicate how potential risk may be assessed. Finally, we consider intervention, both with the suicidal individual and with those relatives who may be bereaved by a person taking his own life.

Suicide and suicidal behaviour in the community

The number of people who successfully kill themselves each year has stabilised and even begun to fall in recent years. However, the incidence of a wide variety of suicidal behaviours has increased markedly and now poses a serious problem for those working in the health and welfare services. Some indication of the size of the problem and its cost can be gained from the fact that among young women self-poisoning is the commonest cause of emergency admission to a hospital ward. It has been estimated that by 1990, if the present trend continues, adults who have poisoned themselves will fill all the available emergency beds.

The profile of those people who actually kill themselves is rather different from that generated by those who attempt to do so — although there is a degree of overlap. Typically the person who commits suicide is male rather than female, and middle-aged or older. Among those engaging in suicide attempts women outnumber men by a ratio of about 2:1. Moreover, the peak years for women are between the years of 15 and 30. Attempting suicide in adolescence appears to have increased in recent years (Kerfoot, 1979). A number of studies conducted in England (Sainsbury, 1955; Bagley, 1973) have indicated that the incidence of suicidal behaviours, like many other forms of social pathology, tend to be concentrated in certain areas of our cities. Typically these are the rather run-down inner city areas, characterised by bed-sitters and multioccupation housing.

The methods by which people take, or attempt to take, their own lives vary. Poisoning by the inhalation of carbon-monoxide contained in coal gas used to be the most common method of suicide. In recent years, coal gas has been replaced by the much safer North Sea gas and now drug-overdosage, sometimes in combination with alcohol, has become the preferred method of the majority. Over 90 per cent of suicide attempts also now involve a drug overdose. In about three-quarters of these instances the drugs involved (frequently tranquillisers) have been prescribed by a doctor. The remainder tend to favour the proprietary medicine (aspirin and paracetamol) readily obtainable from the chemist. The danger of overprescription has received a good deal of attention, in both the specialist medical press and our daily newspapers, over the past few years. It is to be hoped that the message has now got through to all medical practitioners. However, the problem of patients' hoarding tablets is difficult to overcome and social workers should always be alert to this possiblity. If necessary the client may have to be confronted about this, or suspicions communicated to the doctor so that he may examine his own prescribing habits.

Anybody suffering from a psychiatric disorder has an elevated risk of suicide or suicidal behaviour. The most vulnerable group are those suffering from a depressive disorder. The danger is at its most acute when the depression is beginning to lift a little.

Social factors of various kinds appear to play a part in creating the climate for suicidal behaviour. Many of these factors will be very familiar to any social worker, in whatever setting he operates, since in a sense they are his stock-in-trade.

(1) an adverse 'life event' (Paykel *et al.*, 1975) – a personal setback or significant happening which upsets the flow of normal life. Typical of these would be the experience of a major illness or the death of a spouse or other close relative.
(2) 'problems in significant relationships'. These include marital upsets and rows with boy- or girlfriend. Family relationships seem particularly significant in suicide attempts in the young (Kerfoot, 1980).
(3) Employment difficulties also loom large, an increasing

problem in the present economic climate. This appears to be of particular significance to male suicide attempters, almost half of whom, on investigation, have proved to have employment problems.

(4) Social class is also associated with suicidal behaviour. Typically those who attempt suicide come from rather lower social class groups than those who actually take their own lives. The association between lower social class and attempted suicide is echoed by related indicators such as social deprivation, poor housing conditions and impoverished educational facilities.

Finally, it is worth noting that many of those who attempt suicide are already in contact with the health and welfare services. Hawton (1976) has demonstrated that about two-thirds of those people who attempt suicide consult their family doctor in the month before the attempt, frequently, as we have already observed, using the prescribed psychotropic drugs in the subsequent attempt. This being so it is clearly important for social workers, and others, to be able to identify those features in a person's presentation and background which make them a high risk.

The identification of risk

Although, as we have already indicated statistically those who take their own lives and those who merely attempt to do so are rather different groups, there is an overlap. It has been estimated that about 2 per cent of the people who attempt suicide in any given year, will try again *and succeed* within a year of the attempt. The risk of this happening lessens with time but is particularly acute in the first three months following the attempt. Similarly the person who attempts suicide once may attempt again. Estimates place a figure of between 16–25 per cent upon the chances of an individual *repeating the attempt within a year.*

Bearing these facts in mind, it is not surprising that a number of people have tried to develop some method of predicting who is at risk of repeating an attempt and who indeed may succeed next time. Most successful, in terms of predictive power, have been a group of workers in Edinburgh (Buglass and Horton, 1974). They have developed a simple six-item checklist which has proved itself able to predict those most a risk of further attempts. The items they use are as follows:

(a) sociopathy
(b) problem in the use of alcohol
(c) previous psychiatric in—patient care
(d) previous psychiatric out—patient care
(e) previous parasuicide admission (hospital)
(f) not living with a relative.

As with all attempts to simplify reality one is confronted by difficulties of definition. Sociopathy, for example, is defined in this way: 'predominant distress of the patient's situation falls on society'. The definition of 'problem in the use of alcohol' is also rather vague since it includes 'excessive drinking' as well as 'addiction to alcohol' in its definition. Nonetheless, this simple scale, together with an assessment of the individual's own account of the attempt is a useful tool.

The question of intent has been explored by Beck (1974) who suggests that, by careful questionning, some measure of the seriousness of an attempt may be adjudged. He suggests that the interviewer should first focus upon the circumstances of the attempt, taking note of any efforts made to conceal or prepare for the act — writing and leaving of a suicide note for example. Second, he suggests that the individual's own thoughts about the attempt should be elicited, for example, how clearcut was the premeditation, how strongly expressed the wish to die.

Intervention with those who attempt suicide

Because of the deep-seated and wide-ranging nature of the factors involved attempts at the primary prevention of suicide are likely to prove elusive. Clearly, many people would like to see full employment, improved standards of housing and better amenities in inner-city areas. However, it is unlikely that these will be brought about, if at all, with the primary intention of reducing the rate of attempted suicide. Similarly, it is unlikely, however economic circumstances may change, that the course of true love will run smoothly. Claims, made by the Samaritan organisation, as to the part they have played in the prevention and reduction of suicide are rather unrealistic, although it may be true that Samaritans offer comfort to people in distress. The decline is now more generally attributed (Holding, 1974) to the introduction of safer gas supplies and recognition of the dangers of over-prescribing.

Attempts at alleviation are more likely to be successful if they remain focused upon those who have attempted suicide — so-called secondary prevention. This too is problematic. At least initially this relies upon the accurate identification of those who have attempted to kill themselves. Although all suicide attempters, admitted to hospital, are supposed to be seen by a psychiatrist before being discharged, it is clear that for a variety of reasons not all do so. The reasons include pressure upon staff time and patients taking their own early discharge. Indeed one must suppose that only a proportion of suicide attempters reach a hospital in the first place. Nor must it be assumed that suicide attempters will be treated very sympathetically in the context of a general hospital. Ramon (Ramon *et al.*, 1975) has demonstrated how staff in hospitals are sometimes quite hostile and punitive in their dealings with such people. Much as one may regret this, it is understandable how in a busy Casualty Department, over-stretched with roadtraffic accidents, a fairly transparent cry for help — by means of a small overdose — may be treated with little more than a fairly casual administration of a stomach pump. Any work with a person who has attempted suicide should always include some exploration of the possible trauma experienced by the individual in his or her encounters with hospital emergency staff.

Effective intervention must be prefaced by a thorough assessment of the individual concerned and the events surrounding the attempt. Bancroft and Catalan (1978) have developed an assessment interview schedule, which we reproduce as Table 9.1.

Once a thorough assessment has been completed, and some judgment made about the likelihood of a repeat of the suicidal behaviour, the active treatment stage may commence. The evidence for the effectiveness of social work intervention, reviewed by Gibbons (Gibbons *et al.*, 1978) is rather conflicting as few researchers utilised random allocation of clients to experimental and control groups. Gibbons and her colleagues in Southampton, in a carefully

Table 9.1 *Assessment interview*

Establishing rapport	Introduction by name and explanation of the purpose of the interview
Understanding the attempt	Detailed account of events in the 48 hours preceding the attempt
	Circumstances surrounding the act -- degree of planning, isolation, suicide note, motives, actions after attempt, and whether alcohol was taken
	Previous attempts
Clarification of current difficulties	Nature of problems and their duration, and recent changes
	Areas to be covered -- psychological and physical problems, relationship with partner and other family members, children, work, friends and consumption of alcohol
Background	Relevant family and personal history
	Usual personality
Coping	Current coping resources -- personal resources and external resources (such as friends, social agencies, and family doctor)
(Table *cont.* on next page.)	Previous ways of coping with difficulties

Table 9.1 *cont.*

Assessment of mental state at interview	Especially mood and cognitive state
List of current problems	Formulated together with patient
Establishing what further help is required	What the patients wants and is prepared to accept
	Who else should be involved (for example partner or other relatives)
Contract	Terms of further involvement of the assessor or other agencies are made explicit and agreed

Source: Bancroft and Catalan (1978).

organised study, demonstrated that a particular form of social work intervention was capable of affecting some of the underlying social problems and increasing the satisfaction felt by the clients for the service they received. However, their study agrees with an earlier one conducted by Chowdhury (1973), that the intervention was unable to affect the likelihood of repetition of suicial behaviour. It is perhaps worth examining their interventive approach since it is one that we mention elsewhere in the text.

The techniques adopted were developed by Reid (Reid and Epstein, 1972) and are based upon the principle of identifying a limited area of work, accepting an explicit contract, and working within defined time limits. The authors consider that the method is suitable for the following range of problems:

(a) problems of personal relationships
(b) social transitions — losses and changes which impose the necessity of finding new roles
(c) problems in social relations generally
(d) problems of role performance, as a worker, parent etc.
(e) emotional distress interfering with coping ability
(f) problems with officials and organisations
(g) inadequate resources.

Gibbons and her colleagues considered that these areas had much in common with the problems presented by their suicide attempters. Reid specifies a 'problems area' checklist, which was adopted by the research team. Information was then elicited upon each of these areas by the research team. The areas were as follows:

1. *Significant personal relationships:* difficulties in getting on with someone important to the client with whom she was in a continuing personal relationship.
2. *Social transitions:* problems arising from recent or impending changes such as bereavement, break-up of relationships, moving.
3. *Social relations:* loneliness or unsatisfying social life.
4. *Emotional distress* interfering with coping ability.
5. *Practical difficulties:* work, money, or housing.
6. *Problems with formal organisations.*
7. *Domestic difficulties:* problems in role performance as a parent or housewife.

The method, as outlined by Gibbons *et al.*, proceeds in four stages:

1. The range of problems the client perceives in the life areas listed above is explored in order to locate a *target*, that is, the problem perceived as most salient by the client and which he is most motivated to reduce.
2. The goal of treatment is then defined in terms of one or more specific tasks, formulated collaboratively by client and worker. Agreement is reached about the time needed to complete the tasks.
3. The social worker's job is then to help the client to complete the tasks.
4. At termination there is a formal *evaluation* when client and worker discuss what has been achieved and identify further tasks to be undertaken by the client alone.

In evaluating their own work they do not make exaggerated claims for its effectiveness. They conclude:

> we do not know how to prevent people from repeating self-poisoning, but that a planned social work service using a task-

centred approach is more acceptable to patients and can reduce some of their most pressing difficulties in a relatively economical way.

Case example of an elderly person with suicidal behaviour

Mr and Mrs Glasgow, aged 72 and 70 respectively, were a retired professional couple living in a small commuter village about twenty miles from a large city. Their only son was married and living some two hundred miles away. The couple had, until recently, enjoyed an active life sharing a number of leisure pursuits such as golf. Mr Glasgow, an accountant, had retired from his own business at the age of 68, but had retained an interest in it until about eighteen months ago.

Because of the location of their house, their many friends in the city and their golfing interests, they were heavily dependent upon their car, which only Mr Glasgow was able to drive. Mr Glasgow began to suffer a deterioration in his eyesight and this led him to have doubts about his ability to drive. These doubts were confirmed in his mind when he was involved in a slight but potentially fatal accident. After the accident Mr Glasgow became preoccupied with his health, and his wife noted that he had become anxious and uneasy. He was persuaded to visit his doctor who prescribed some medication to ease the feelings of anxiety. He curtailed his driving and a sense of isolation began to develop, although his wife attempted to help him overcome this.

A crisis occurred wheen he was brought home in a very distressed state after a further accident. The doctor was called and Mr Glasgow broke down and quite spontaneously said that it had not been an accident, but that he had tried to kill himself. The doctor offered Mr Glasgow a bed at a local hospital for a few days, where a course of anti-depressant drugs was started.

At this point a social worker became involved and on visiting Mrs Glasgow soon became aware that she harboured a good deal of unexpressed resentment about her husband's behaviour. Mrs Glasgow's anger centred on her feelings of rejection: 'How could he do this to me, how could he leave me?'

After a few days in hospital Mr Glasgow was discharged and the social worker saw them both and arranged to see them together for a further six sessions in order to attempt to resolve some of their problems. Mr Glasgow's mood state had begun to improve, but Mrs Glasgow had begun to think seriously about leaving her husband and was herself becoming agitated and mildly depressed.

After the first of the six planned sessions the social worker drew up a list of what they saw to be the areas that required attention:

(a) both Mr and Mrs Glasgow had a growing sense of isolation.
(b) their car represented (particularly to Mr Glasgow) independence and its loss was associated with his own ageing.
(c) Mr Glasgow had feelings of worthlessness related to this ageing and to the loss of his former role in his business.
(d) Mrs Glasgow was feeling rejected by her husband.
(e) little direct communication on an emotional level took place between them and the social worker had the potential role of interpreter between them.

The family practitioner meanwhile continued the programme of medication for Mr Glasgow. In the five sessions now remaining the social worker began to examine some of the emotional and practical issues involved, helping each to see how he or she contributed to the problems.

It became clear that if they remained in their present house without a car their social isolation would increase. In turn this would result in their spending more time alone together and thus exacerbating their other interpersonal problems. Some of these had existed for many years, but in better times had remained dormant. Moving into the city was discussed, but this would have left them short of capital. A number of other housing options were discussed, including what the social worker thought an ill-advised idea of sharing a house with their son. The social worker introduced them to a leasehold sheltered housing scheme, run by a housing association. This it was felt would offer a number of advantages: it was close to friends, public transport and golf-courses; it would enable them to retain some of their capital and offer the opportunity for neighbourly contacts and, at some future date, the benefits of a warden and an alarm system should they be required.

The loss of the car still left Mr Glasgow feeling depressed and to an extent unable to offer much else to the running of the household. Alternative ways in which he might contribute, both within the home and in the wider community were discussed.

For Mrs Glasgow her husband's action had reactivated feelings long buried within their marriage about her own vulnerability. It had also brought home to her how dependent she was upon her husband and how in the normal course of events she might well be left as a widow.

At the end of the five working sessions the couple were talking more openly about their fears, beginning to appreciate a little better each others feelings, and thinking positively about a move into the city.

At follow-up after eight months the move to a small leasehold sheltered housing scheme had been made. Mr Glasgow was active with the residents' association, and was currently negotiating with a tour operator a holiday at reduced rates to Portugal for himself, his wife and a party of tenants. Mrs Glasgow, whilst still concerned about her husband's future health, had strengthened her many friendships in golfing circles and was waiting to be given a lift in order to compete in the weekly medal competition. One of her closest friends had recently been widowed and Mrs Glasgow had been able to offer a lot of support, whilst Mr Glasgow had helped in sorting out the will and tangle over some insurance policies.

Social work and the bereaved

Social work involvement with suicidal behaviour need not be confined to those people who survive an attempt. A group of people who tend to be overlooked are those who suffer bereavement because of the death of a spouse or other relative. Shepherd and Barraclough (1979) have sensitively highlighted, what they regard as an area of unmet need by talking with a group of people who had suffered the loss of a husband or wife by suicide. They draw, in their work, upon studies by Morris and Parkes (Parkes, 1975) both of whom have been concerned to understand the impact of bereavement upon the individual.

Shepherd and Barraclough identify six broad categories of possible need: practical, financial, comfort and support, advice and information, religious counselling, and other kinds of need. Although 42 per cent of the suicide cases studied had in fact died in hospital, none of the surviving spouses who were interviewed, reported having had any contact with the hospital social worker — this in spite of the fact that many of the victims had been previously receiving hospital treatment for illness, much of it psychiatric.

Shepherd and Barraclough report upon the importance of what they term a 'psychological autopsy'. Helping the bereaved partner systematically to discuss the events leading up to the suicide, the emotional reaction and subsequent adjustment to it. Their work leads them to suggest that, in every case of suicide, the next-of-kin should be referred to the hospital social work department or that a special social worker should be attached to the coroner's court. They estimate that in the majority of cases only one visit, by the social worker, would be required. Factual information could be given and reassurance obtained that the person concerned had adequate support available in the form of friends or relatives. In the minority of instances these social supports may be lacking, in which case a more lengthy social work intervention may be indicated. For a fuller discussion of work with the bereaved readers are recommended to an excellent book by Carole Smith (1982).

Conclusion

Suicide and suicidal behaviour poses for the social worker both practical and emotional problems. It is difficult to remain unmoved when those with whom one works attempt, and succeed, in taking their own lives. Nor is this simply a pressure that one is likely to receive from clients. The feeling that one ought to take one's own life is surprisingly widespread and suicide is highest in many of those jobs which are emotionally demanding. It has been estimated that one male doctor in every fifty ends his life by killing himself. Within that professional grouping psychiatrists are particularly vulnerable, as is anybody who shares the distress of the mentally ill.

We have already indicated the order of practical problems presented by suicidal behaviour. However, it is possible to consider these dilemmas on a rather different plane. The issue then becomes one of what right the worker has to intervene, what right he has to stop somebody taking his own life. Do social workers risk undermining more general freedoms if they insist upon controlling somebody's albeit self-destructive behaviour? As the French novelist and philosopher, Albert Camus (1975), points out, knowing that one has the power to end one's own life at any time, gives one the freedom to live.

10

The Mental Health Act Legislation

At the time it was introduced in 1959 the Mental Health Act was seen as heralding a new era of psychiatric treatment and care. It was a time of great optimism within the discipline of psychiatry with the belief that community care, together with psychotropic drugs would reduce the need for institutional treatment. It was felt that psychiatric knowledge and techniques had advanced sufficiently for them to take their place alongside the other medical disciplines.

In the wake of the optimism the 1959 Act sought to remove the magistrate from the process of compulsory committal. The central tenet of the Act was the belief that most treatment should be offered on either a voluntary basis to in-patients or to people remaining in the community as out-patients.

The framers of the Act acknowledged that not all mental illness could be treated in this way, and that in some cases, when the individual was either a danger to himself or to others, compulsory powers should be retained. However, it was felt that the medical profession, acting in a spirit of goodwill, should be allowed to exercise these powers unhampered by legal procedures. Initially the legislative changes met with few criticisms. However, there has developed recently something of a campaign to re-examine some of the original tenets of the Act and recast them. Concern has focused on the way in which the compulsory powers may be abused and more particularly the way in which the Mental Health Review Tribunal goes about its work of dealing with subsequent appeals against compulsory hospitalisation. While something under 10 per cent of the psychiatric hospital population are detained under a section of the Mental Health Act, there are worrying regional variations which suggest that different practices prevail. Moreover, it has been suggested that the mere presence of compulsory powers may be sufficient to persuade people to enter hospital who might otherwise be reluctant to do so. Hospital social workers will know from their own experience how the patient, once in hospital, may be led to believe that he is still being detained under one of the sections of the Act even though it may already have lapsed. Similarly, informal patients may be threatened with the possiblity of 'being put on a section' should they prove troublesome to staff. The Act may therefore be a powerful agent of control even without its formal invocation. Some hospitals, conscious of this possibility, now issue patients with a letter informing them that they have been admitted under Section 25 or 26 (2 and 3 in the 1983 Act) and informing them of their rights with regard to an appeal.

The wider debate, raising as it does complex issues of civil liberty and medical ethics, cannot adequately be aired in a book such as this. However, anybody who in the course of his work has to deal with either mental illness or the formal legislation which surrounds it should become involved in the issues. MIND (the National Association of Mental Health) has been particularly active in this field (see Gostin, 1977).

The debate, sparked off by concern about the implementation of the 1959 Act, led to two government publications. The first, a consultation paper, was published by the DHSS in 1976; this was followed in 1978 by a government white paper entitled *Review of the Mental Health Act*. Olsen (1982) suggests that five main principles prompted the campaign for reform. These were as follows:

> that all mentally disordered people may legitimately expect that their rights will be safeguarded; that the procedures for effecting a compulsory admission will be carried out within the regulations and spirit of the law; that compulsory care should be in the least restrictive conditions possible; that the professionals concerned with their treatment and care are adequately trained and their competence assessed; and that the quality of care and treatment does not fall below the accepted minimum.

Both documents and the discussion they in turn engendered have led to a series of amendments to the Bill, passed in 1982. These go some way towards meeting some of the injustices surrounding the rights of patients, and also attempt to tighten up professional practice. However, they fall short of the demands made by MIND and others for more far-reaching reforms.

What follows is a review of the amended 1959 Mental Health Act focused upon those sections which most concern social workers. The Royal Assent was given to the Mental Health (Amendment) Bill in October 1982, and the consolidating Bill was passed in the spring of 1983. The new Bill has revised the numbers for the various sections, and these are provided in brackets.

In one of their contributions to the wider debate the British Association of Social Workers outlined the role and duty of a social worker with regard to the Act as it affects his clients. These are:

1. To investigate the patient's social situation and to identify, in consultation with others involved, the extent to which social and environmental pressures have contributed to his observed behaviour;
2. To use his professional skills to help resolve any social relationship or environmental difficulties which have contributed to the crisis, and to mobilise community resources appropriately;
3. To be familiar with legal requirements and to ensure that they are fulfilled;
4. To form his own opinions, after interviews with the patient, those closest to him and others involved, as to whether or not compulsory admission is necessary, after consideration of any alternative methods of resolving the crisis, and securing the necessary care or treatment;
5. To ensure that care and treatment are offered in the least restrictive conditions possible.

The Mental Health Act

The Act begins by establishing four categories of mental disorder:

(a)   mental illness
(b)   mental impairment, involving significant impairment of intelligence and social functioning
(c)   severe mental impairment involving severe impairment of intelligence and social functioning
(d)   psychopathic disorder, 'a persistent disorder or disability of mind which results in abnormally aggressive or seriously irresponsible conduct'.

The definitions offered are by no means clear. Mental illness is not defined at all, while psychopathy or personality disorder, which some consider should not be included in this rubric at all, are at best very loose terms. Psychopathy is a state about which there is no general agreement and for which there is no recognised or effective treatment available. And yet included within the Act for those deemed to fall within categories (b), (c) and (d) and whose impairment is 'associated with abnormally aggressive or seriously irresponsible conduct' there is the proviso that they should not be detained in hospital unless 'such treatment is likely to alleviate or prevent a deterioration in condition'.

This new phrase is intended to provide a more strict criterion for treatability. However, it is open to various interpretations, and only after some years of practice are we likely to discover if this has resulted in more or less people being detained in hospital.

Applications for admission or guardianship

The 1959 Act imposed upon mental welfare officers a duty to use their own judgment in respect of an application for compulsory admission to hospital (Section 54, now 13). This required that they not only ensured that the legal requirements of the Act relating to the application had been complied with, but that, having regard to all the circumstances including the contents of the medical recommendation, it is, in the words of the Act, 'necessary or proper' for the application to be made. This dual obligation will now be passed, under the amended legislation, to an 'approved social worker' who must interview the patient and satisfy himself that detention in hospital is the most appropriate way of providing care and treatment. The 'approved social worker' concept will not become operative until October 1984. By that time CCETSW will have established a system of validating social workers, who must have undergone a further period of specialist in-service training.

Section 25 (2)

This section of the Act allows a patient to be detained in a hospital for a period of 28 days for assessment purposes. Two medical opinions are required prior to this detainment, and in their view the patient should be suffering from a mental disorder of specified kind and the detention must be necessary for his own health or safety, or the protection of others.

One of the two medical practitioners must be approved by a local health authority as having special experience in the diagnosis or treatment of mental disorder. Three other conditions pertain to the medical staff: they must have examined the individual either at the same time or within an interval of not more than five days; only one recommendation may come from a doctor on the full-time staff of the hospital to which the patient is to be admitted, and no recommendation may be given by a doctor who has any personal relationship to or with the patient.

The recent amendments do provide two extra safeguards for the patient. The first is that he will be given the opportunity to appeal against detention to a Mental Health Review Tribunal within the first 14 days of the detention. The second is that the nearest relative is given a discharge power, subject to the limitations inherent in Section 48 (23, 25), where the Responsible Medical Officer (RMO) considers the patient to be dangerous.

Section 26 (3)

Section 26 (3) allows the detention of a patient for up to a period of six months under the same conditions as Section 25 (2). This may be extended by a further six months, and then by periods of one year at a time. In the case of a recommendation for treatment, the social worker should, wherever possible, consult with the nearest relative prior to making the application, and must not proceed if the relative raises any objection. An application to the county court would be necessary to overrule this. For the purposes of the Act, a cohabitee who has lived with the patient for five years counts as the 'nearest relative'. The recommendation from the doctors must state the particular grounds for the treatment order and specify why no other method of dealing with the patient is deemed to be appropriate.

The so-called 'treatability test' in this section of the Act is intended to ensure that only those people who would actually benefit from any treatment given may be detained. From September 1983 'it shall be the duty of the District Health Authority and of the local social services authority to provide, in co-operation with relevant voluntary agencies, aftercare services' for any patient who has been detained under Sections 26, 60, 72 or 73 (3, 37, 47, 48) until the DHA or SSD 'are satisfied that the person concerned is no longer in need of such services'.

Section 29 (4)

Section 29 (4) of the Act, which allows for emergency admissions for up to three days, has come in for particular criticism. It appears to have been very unevenly used throughout the country and could, if sufficient crisis teams existed, be used even less.

Admission follows the recommendation of any one doctor, as long as it is supported by an approved social worker or the *nearest* relative. The person making the application should have seen the individual within the previous 24 hours.

The intention has always been that this section of the Act should be used only in extreme emergencies. However, the suspicion has developed that its use, relying upon only one doctor, has grown to suit medical convenience. As Olsen (1981) comments:

> the use of this section deprives a patient of his primary safeguard, a psychiatric and social work opinion, and risks the continuance of a psychiatric practice based on what is convenient for the doctors rather than on what is necessary for patients' rights and well-being.

Section 30 (5)

This section allows a hospital doctor, either the patient's own or one nominated to act on his behalf, to detain a previously informal patient for a maximum of 72 hours. If no doctor is immediately available, a nurse may detain a patient for six hours until a doctor is available.

Section 33 (7)

A person aged over 16 may be received into the guardianship of an individual or the social services department where this is considered to be 'in the interests of the welfare of the patient'. The conditions under which an application and recommendation are made are similar to those for Section 26 (3). The powers of the guardian are now much more specific than those under the original (1959) legislation, which gave powers similar to those of a parent of a child under 14. They now allow the guardian to require that the patient live in a specified place and attend for medical treatment, occupation, education or training. The guardian may also require access for specified persons to see the patient.

Section 60 (37)

This section enables a hospital or guardianship order to be made if, following conviction for an offence punishable with imprisonment, two doctors state that the offender is suffering from one of the conditions defined in the Act of such a nature or degree as to warrant reception into guardianship or detention for medical treatment. A hospital must be willing to accept the individual or the local services department or named individual be prepared to receive him into guardianship. The court must also be of the view that this course of action represents the most suitable method of dealing with the case.

Section 65 (41)

A restriction order may be made in addition to a hospital order by the Crown Court if the latter thinks that this is necessary for the protection of the public from serious harm, bearing in mind 'the nature of the offence, the antecedents of the offender, and the risk of his committing further offences if set at large'. The patient in such an event may only be allowed his liberty with the consent of the Secretary of State or by a Mental Health Review Tribunal. Social workers may be asked to supervise patients in the community who have been discharged from hospital but who remain subject to certain restrictions under this section.

Sections 72 and 73 (47, 48)

These sections allow for a person who is already in custody, either awaiting trial or serving a sentence, whose mental state becomes such that he requires compulsory detention in hospital to be transferred.

Section 135 (135)

Where a social worker has reasonable cause to suspect that a mentally disordered person is being ill-treated, neglected or is not cared for properly (by himself if living alone), he can lay information on oath before a Justice of the Peace and obtain a warrant for a constable to enter and search premises, and, if necessary, to remove the patient to a place of safety.

Social reports (14)

In cases where the nearest relative makes the application, for a patient to be admitted to hospital the managers of the hospital will notify the social services department, and a social worker will interview the patient and prepare a report for the managers on the patient's social circumstances. This is a new provision and its impact will vary according to existing practices.

Section 136 (136)

This allows a police officer, should he find somebody in a public place suffering from a mental disorder and in need of care or control, to take that person to a 'place of safety'. This means in practice a police station, a residential home or a hospital. The person may be detained for no more than 72 hours. The person should during this time be examined by a doctor and interviewed by a social worker so that any necessary arrangements for treatment or care may be made.

Consent to treatment

This section of the Amendment Bill was one of the most controversial and eventually a compromise package was agreed upon. The new provisions do not apply to patients on short-term detention orders or on remand for reports, but do include Section 26 (3) patients on leave of absence. Treatments requiring consent and or a second opinion do not include urgent treatments which are life-saving or immediately necessary to prevent violence, a serious deterioration in the patient's condition or to alleviate serious suffering.

This is clearly a complicated area and one that is still likely to be open to interpretation and therefore controversy. The following three points are worth highlighting:

1. Certain treatments will require consent *and* a second opinion. These will include psychosurgery and other treatments, as yet unspecified by the Secretary of State. Patients, in order to give their consent, should be 'capable

of understanding the nature, purpose and likely effects of the treatment'.

2. Some treatments will require consent *or* a second opinion. These treatments will include ECT, medication and 'such other forms of treatment and diagnostic procedures as may be specified in Regulations'. For these treatments, if a patient does not consent or is incapable of consenting, a second medical opinion will be necessary and the independent doctor will be required to consult a nurse and one other professional person concerned with the patient's treatment. This does not apply, however, to medicines (other than those in Regulations) given in the first three months following detention.

3. Where the Secretary of State has not specified that a particular form of treatment should come under one of the first two headings than no consent will be required if treatment is given under the direction of the responsible medical officer.

The Mental Health Act Commission

The Mental Health Act Commission is a multi-disciplinary health authority whose job is to monitor the workings of the Act. Its two main functions are:

(a) to inspect and review the care of detained patients and, where necessary, investigate patients' complaints

(b) appoint the doctors and other persons necessary to provide an independent second opinion in cases where this is needed before treatment can be given.

The role of the Commission may be extended to include informal patients.

The Mental Health Review Tribunal

The Mental Health Review Tribunal is an independent body whose task is to consider requests from detained patients for discharge into the community. Patients may apply for review or this may be automatic if they either fail to make application in the first six months of detention or have not been reviewed for three years. In recent years social workers have become involved with helping patients present their case to the tribunal. A useful practical guide to this process is now available from MIND (Gostin and Rassaby, 1981). A significant increase in the number of tribunals may be anticipated in the future and so social workers should familiarise themselves with their operation.

The role of the social worker

The part played by social workers in using the Mental Health Act has come in for increased scrutiny. It was recognised in the 1981 White Paper that the social worker has a 'key role in considering compulsory admission to hospital'. However, since the absorption of the specialist mental welfare officer into the social services department following the Seebohm reorganisation, much of this expertise has been dissipated.

The concept of the 'approved social worker' (which comes into force in October 1984) working within a generic department is an attempt to recapture something of that specialisation. Qualified social workers will have to undergo a further period of specialist training and/or assessment, in order to be able to operate the powers inherent in the Act that relate to compulsory detention and guardianship.

The social worker has an obligation, if admission is being considered, not only to interview the would-be patient in a suitable manner, but also to satisfy himself that compulsory detention in a hospital is the most appropriate step. When family and doctor may be pressing the need for hospitalisation it may be difficult to resist. It seems apparent that the decision-making is shaped by a whole series of extraneous social factors. In a study of compulsory admissions in an area of London, Szmukler *et al.* (1981) concluded that the following set of circumstances made a compulsory admission more likely to occur:

(a) a very disturbed patient who was often incoherent and unable to give a reliable account of himself
(b) an out-of-hours emergency with attendant difficulties

in obtaining information from hospital, social services, etc.

(c) the crisis often occurred in a public place where the situation could not be contained long enough for more information to become available and thereby permit the consideration of an alternative course to admission — for example, in a hotel

(d) the absence of a friend or relative who knew the patient

(e) professionals involved on an emergency basis with no previous knowledge of the patient

(f) although in half of the cases the patient's attitude to the prospect of admission was not in doubt, in a substantial proportion it was ambiguous, leaving the assessors in a dilemma as to how much pressure they could legitimately bring to bear on the patient to move him to hospital.

This work succinctly points out the complexities of the issues involved and indicates the need for better follow-up, after care and the development of proper crisis teams.

Conclusion

It is not surprising, given the extent of the powers extended to professionals under the Mental Health Act, that Olsen (1981) has commented that they are 'powers which have no parallel in law and which deprive the mentally disordered person of virtually all safeguards available to those who are not disordered'. It is with this knowledge that social workers should approach every potential mental health crisis. In the absence of genuine community alternatives, the social worker often has no other recourse but to make use of compulsory powers. But in doing so he should ensure that not only the letter of the law is being applied but that both the wishes of the family and the patient have been taken into account. Decision-making in this area is always likely to appear rather messy to the outsider. When so many conflicting interests — personal liberty, safety of individuals, etc. — have to be reconciled, we have to rely for good practice upon adequate training and good faith.

Conclusion

The granting of the Royal Assent to the Mental Health (Amendment) Bill brings to a close a recent round of debate about the care of the mentally ill. The establishment of an 'approved social worker' will undoubtedly affect not only the way in which the service is offered to the mentally disordered but influence more general changes in social work.

The 'approved social worker' needs to consider what are the central aims of social work with the mentally ill? We have suggested that as mental disorders, irrespective of diagnostic category, disrupt psychosocial functioning, then any form of social care must attempt to focus upon these difficulties. Consequently social workers need to be equipped with knowledge and skills that facilitate the client's ability to establish and maintain communication with those about them. This necessitates the social worker being able to utilise, or at least be familiar with, techniques of intervention as varied as chemotherapy and family therapy. On the current evidence, this leads us to advocate the use of an integrated and eclectic form of social work such as we describe in Chapters 2 to 4. In order to optimise this approach, work within a multi-disciplinary team is advisable. This means that the social worker has a responsibility to work and liaise with related professions.

The changing role of social work with mentally ill people

We began this Conclusion by referring to the Mental Health

Act amendments, which we detail in Chapter 10. The discussions which surrounded these amendments may be linked with those which accompanied the publication of the Barclay Report (1982) which sought to review the role of social work in the contemporary world. Both, we believe, presage changes in the role of social workers with mentally ill people.

As we indicated earlier, the amendments to the Mental Health Act go some way·to meet those critics who called for tighter legal control, greater emphasis upon patients rights and the closure of certain legal loopholes. However, we share the concern of Olsen (1982) that the attention which has been paid to the rights issues, has deflected attention away from the fundamental issue of resources. For example, the question of compulsory admission is always going to prove problematic whatever legal safeguards are devised. But these dilemmas may be eased if alternatives to hospitals are provided, the social worker involved is adequately trained and supported, or a fully-fledged crisis team is on hand to attend to the client in his own home. In the concentration upon legal niceties the government may have been allowed to escape from the responsibility of adequately funding community-based resources which might offer genuine alternatives to hospitalisation.

The Barclay Report too was concerned about clients' rights and saw merit in the devopment of some specialist roles within the social work team. The question seems to be, how narrowly does one define these specialisms? Nobody, would surely now wish to seek a return to the pre-Seebohm days of child care, mental health and welfare specialisms? However, we have long advocated the need (Pritchard and Butler, 1976) for some specialist mental health training for social workers. Whilst supporting the notion of the generic team, we feel that there is a place for somebody who wishes to develop special interests and skills and who may develop a caseload to reflect this. They may receive direct referrals which have an obvious mental health component or act as consultants on mental health matters for the wider team.

The Barclay Report and the amended Mental Health Act, are clear reaffirmations of the need for care in the community. The Barclay Report also called for a widening of the social work role, embracing, some elements of community work. The so-called 'community social worker' who would emerge would have, as well as a counselling role, one which involved generating community resources and stimulating self-help networks. The picture painted is an attractive one in which the social worker, acting as catalyst, draws out of the community those natural resources which may exist to help and support the vulnerable. Despite the seductive presentation in the majority report of Barclay, the trenchant criticisms of Pinker contained in the minority report, must not be ignored. A further note of caution must be struck with regard to the mentally ill. Will support be so readily forthcoming from the community should the neighbourhood model be adopted for them? The evidence is (Pritchard and Cuncliffe, 1983) that the general public still retain many of their negative stereotypes about mental illness and may be unwilling to extend the kind of support envisages by Barclay towards this client group?

We have in embryo, the potential for a greatly improved service for those who are mentally ill. The large Victorian asylums have been reduced in size, albeit more slowly than many had hoped or predicted. Many psychiatric out-patient clinics have been moved to the more centrally located general hospitals. A new generation of family practitioners is emerging from our medical schools, better trained and more interested in mental health problems than ever before. Social work has expanded rapidly over the past twenty years, and the quality of entrants is high; many social services departments are close to having the majority of their field staff qualified. Nursing too has changed, and the shift in emphasis towards the community is reflected by the growth of community psychiatric nurses.

We have a solid commitment to develop care in the community and various models have been developed, on a pilot basis, to demonstrate how this might work effectively. However, community care is not a cheap option. It can, in the long-term, prove more cost-effective than hospitalisation. What we now require is that the rhetoric of community care be backed up by more resources. These resources we suggest, need to go in the following directions. Specialist training, as advocated in the Mental Health Amendment Act, should be given to social workers to enhance their effectiveness and encourage them to take on mental health cases. Increased efforts should be made to develop more group homes and other housing alternatives such as sheltered housing and boarding-out schemes. More day centres are required to provide purposive activity for the sufferers and respite for their families. Shop front drop-in centres should be developed to offer advice and support without the necessity of having to consult a doctor. Finally, we would like to see the development of psychiatric crisis teams which could offer a genuine alternative to compulsory hospitalisation and help people to face up to crisis in their own homes.

If these steps were taken we believe that public attitudes would begin to change, as fewer mentally ill people would be shut away and more would be seen to cope adequately in the community. Only then might we get the wholehearted neighbourhood and family support that would see an end to those mental health casualties who have been left 'like shadows, wandering in the day'.

Appendices

I

A Proposed Social History Outline to Provide Basic Information

It must be stressed that it is not expected that the social worker would gain all this information on the initial contact with the client or family, but the following lists are areas of possible relevance dependent upon the nature of the difficulties the client is experiencing.

Age and sex   Behaviour is often age- and sex-related.

Marital status

Current address   Living where and with whom.

Informant   Is information gained from the indexed person or a member of his family. It is important to note the relationship of any person who is not 'the indexed client' and the state of the relationship between the informant and the patient.

Current family situation   Ages and names of spouse and children. It is important here to notice different possible impacts. Note also if there is a previous family of an earlier marriage etc.

Any relevant previous family history   i.e. with parents or siblings. A number of studies have indicated that certain types of mental disorder are familial.

Presenting problem

What is the client, his family and/or others complaining of?
What appears to be the difficulty?
When did it start?
What if any are the precipitant factors?
What are his characteristic patterns of behaviour, before and since the problem?
Who referred the client and why?
How frequently, if at all, has the client been known to the agency previously?

Social factors

Education   Achievements and background.

Work Current and recent record. Note any changes over the last six months.
Housing Type. Note again any changes over the last six months.
Social amenities Rural, inner city etc.

Personal factors

Family relationships
Impact of the problem on the family If there is a previous episode note possible change in family responses to the present difficulty.
Describe any other significant relationships e.g. close friends, elderly parents, etc.

Previous psychosocial history

Number of hospital admissions and possible reasons.
Previous mental illness, suicidal behaviour, offences, other kinds of problems
NB Are there any changes in the current presenting problem from what might have gone before?
Physical factors. Note general state of health.

Personality

Tentative description of personaal characteristics of the individual with special emphasis upon personality style prior to present difficulty.

Work of immediate priority – plan and discuss with client

(a) Emotional
(b) Material/Income
(c) Social
(d) Physical

II

Drugs

Approved name	Commercial name	Side-effects
Major tranquillisers		
Chlorpromazine	Largactil	A sedative effect which may produce drowsiness
Haloperidol	Serenace Haldol	The others are less sedating but produce more unpleasant side-effects — Parkinsonism, restlessness, postural hypotension, etc.
Perphenazine	Fentazin	
Promazine	Sparine	
Thioridazine	Melleril	
Trifluoperazine	Stelazine	
Eluphenazine Enanthate	Moditen	Long-acting often called 'depot injections'. Similar side-effects to the above.
Fluphenazine Decanoate	Modecate	
Fluphenthixol Decanoate	Depixol	
Clopenthixol	Clopixol	
Minor tranquillisers		
Chlordiazepoxide	Librium	Drowsiness, dizziness, dependence may develop in high doses
Diazepam	Valium	
Lorazepam	Ativan	
Oxazepam	Serenid–D	
Hypnotics		
Flurazepam	Dalmane	Side-effects shared with minor tranquillisers
Nitrapepam	Mogadon	
Temazepam	Normison	
Triazolam	Halcion	

Approved name	*Commercial name*	*Side-effects*
Antidepressants		
Tricyclics		
Amitriptyline	Tryptizol	
	Lentizol	Dryness of mouth
Clomipramine	Anafranil	tiredness, sweating,
Imipramine	Tofranil	constipation

Monoamine oxidase inhibitors (MAOI)

Phenelzine	Nardil	Dizziness, hypotension, blurred vision
Isocarboxazid	Marplan	Dry mouth, dizziness,
Tranylcypromine	Parnate	hypotension

Lithium

Lithium carbonate	Priadel	Tremor, loss of appetite, thirst and dryness of mouth

III

Some Useful Addresses

Army Benevolent Fund, Dept. C, Duke of Yorks, H.Q., Chelsea, London, SW3. Telephone: 01–730–5388.

Age Concern, Bernard Sunley House, 60 Pitcairn Road, Mitcham, Surrey. Telephone: 01–640–5431.

Alcoholics Anonymous (AA), PO Box 514, 11 Redcliffe Road, London, SW10.

British Association of Behavioural Psychotherapy. Sec: W.W. Lomas, Social Services Dept: Craig House, Bank St., Bury, BL9 0BA.

DHSS, Alexander Fleming House, Elephant and Castle, London, SE1 6BY.

Ex-Services Mental Welfare Society, Baltic Chambers, 3 Cadogant, Glasgow, G2. Telephone: 041–221–1303.

MIND (National Association for Mental Health), 22 Harley Street, London, W1M 2ED.

National Schizophrenia Fellowship, 79 Victoria Road, Surbiton, Surrey. Telephone: 01–390–3651/2/3.

Phobics Society, 4 Cheltenham Road, Manchester, M21. Telephone: 061–881–1937.

Psychiatric Rehabilitation Association, 21a Kingsland High Street, London, E8. Telephone: 01–254–9753.

Richmond Fellowship, 8 Addison Road, London, W14. Telephone: 01–603–6373.

Royal Air Force Association, 43 Grove Park Road, London, W4. Telephone: 01–994–8504.

Royal British Legion, 49 Pall Mall, London, SW1. Telephone: 01–930–8135.

Royal Naval Benevolent Society, 1 Fleet Street, London, EC4. Telephone: 01–353–9565.

Samaritans, 17 Uxbridge Road, Slough, Berks. Telephone: 0753–32713.

Schizophenia Association of Great Britain, TyrTwr, Llanfair Hall, Caernafun, Gwynedd. Telephone: 0248–670379.

Society of St Vincent de Paul, 24 George Street, London, W1. Telephone: 01–935–7625.

Further Reading

Chapter 1   What is Meant by Mental Illness

There are a number of basic psychiatric texts available, among them those by Curran *et al*. (1975), Hamilton (1978) and Linford-Rees (1970). A recent book written with social workers in mind is that by Hudson (1982). For a review of the controversy surrounding the medical model the books by Clare (1976) and Wing (1978) are recommended. A trenchant look at some of psychiatry's critics is provided by Sedgwick (1982).

Chapter 2   The Impact of Mental Disorder

Britain is a multiracial society and many of our responses to mental illness are coloured by the particular culture in which we are brought up. A valuable insight into the presentation and meaning of mental illness among the ethnic minorities in Britain is provided by *Aliens and Alienists: Ethnic Minorities and Psychiatry* (Littlewood and Lipsedge, 1982).

Chapter 5   Different Approaches to Work with Mentally Disordered People

A good introduction to family therapy is provided by Sue Walrond-Skinner (1976) and Robin Skynner (1976). Two books which may be recommended as an introduction to individual psychotherapy are those by Bloch (1979) and Sandler (1973). Finally, for those wishing to incorporate behavioural strategies into their work an excellent introduction is provided by Fischer and Gochros (1975).

Chapter 6   Social Work and Schizophrenia: a Case Study

A very useful overview of schizophrenia is provided by Andrew Smith

(1982). This book might well meet the needs of relatives anxious to learn more about the disorder. Another with very similar objectives is *Understanding and Helping the Schizophrenic: a guide for family and friends* by Silvano Arieti (1979).

Chapter 7   Drugs and Physical Treatment

The best simple guide to drugs used in psychiatry is that by Crammer, Barraclough and Heine (1978).

Chapter 8   Psychiatric Emergencies

For an introduction to dealing with a psychiatric emergency the best book is still that by Caplan (1964), *Principles of Preventive Psychiatry*.

Chapter 10   The Mental Health Act Legislation

The general historical background to the Mental Health Act and the development of services is provided by Jones (1972). The two books by Gostin (1977) and (1981), written for MIND, are both extremely useful guides to legislation as is Bean's well researched book (1980) on compulsory admissions to hospital. Books by Edwards (1976) and Hoggett (1976) provide useful guidance upon matters of Law. This chapter has concentrated upon the Mental Health Act, but social workers should also be aware of other legislation which has implications for the mentally ill. The Chronically Sick and Disabled Persons Act (1970), the National Health Service Act 1977 (especially schedule 8, which refers to the provision of various services) and the National Assistance Act 1948 (which includes the duty to protect the property of people admitted to hospital) all give the social worker powers and duties. An excellent source of reference for these and other areas is provided by the comprehensive *Encyclopaedia of Social Services Law and Practice* by Jones (1982).

Bibliography

Apte, R.Z. (1968) *Halfway Houses*, London, Bell.

Arieti, S. (1979) *Understanding and Helping the Schizophrenic: a Guide for Family and Friends*, Harmondsworth, Penguin.

Bagley, C. *et al.* (1973) 'Social structure and the ecological distribution of mental illness, suicide and delinquency', *Psychological Medicine* 3, 2.

Baker, R. (1976) *The Interpersonal Process in Generic Social Work*, Bundoora, Australia, PIT Press.

Baker, R. (1971) 'Use of operant conditioning to reinstate speech in mute schizophrenics', *Behavioural Research and Therapy*, 9, pp. 326—9.

Bancroft, J.H.J. and Catalan, J. (1978) 'Assessment of patients following self-poisoning or self-injury', Oxford University, Department of Psychiatry, Unpublished.

Barclay Report (1982) *Social Workers: Their Role and Tasks*, London, National Institute of Social Work, and Bedford Square Press.

Bateson, G., Jackson, D., Haley, J. and Weakland, J. (1956) 'Towards a theory of schizophrenia, *Behavioural Science*, 1, pp. 251— 64.

Bean, P. (1980) *Compulsory Admission to Mental Hospitals*, London, John Wiley.

Beck, A.T. *et al.* (1961) 'An inventory for measuring depression', *Archives of General Psychiatry*, 4, pp. 561—571.

Beck, A.T., Shuyler D. and Herman, I. (1974) *The Prediction of Suicide*, New York, Charles Press.

Beck, A.T. (1967) *Depression: Clinical, Experimental and Theoretical Aspects*, New York, Hoeber.

Beck, A.T. Rush, J. Shaw, B. and Emery, G. (1979) *Cognitive Therapy of Depression*, New York, Wiley.

Bellak, L. (1958) *Schrizophrenia*, New York, Basic Books.

Blackburn, I.M. *et al.* (1981) 'The efficacy of cognitive therapy in depression: a treatment trial using cognitive therapy and pharmaco-therapy, each alone and in combination', *British Journal of Psychiatry*, 139, pp. 181—9.

Bloch, S. (ed.) (1979) *An Introduction to the Psychotherapies*, Oxford University Press.

Braun, P. *et al.* (1981) 'An overview: de-institutionalisation of psychiatric patients: a critical review of outcome studies', *American Journal of Psychiatry*, 138 (6), pp. 736–49.

Brearley, C.P. (1982) *Risk and Social Work*, London, Routledge & Kegan Paul.

Brewer, C. and Lait, J. (1980) *Can Social Work Survive?* London, Martin Robertson.

Brown, G.W. (1959) 'Experiences of discharged chronic schizophrenic patients in various types of living group', *Millbank Memorial Fund Quarterly*, 37, pp. 105–31.

Brown, G.W., Birley, J.L.T. and Wing, J.K. (1972) 'Influence of family life on the course of schizophrenic disorders: a replication', *British Journal of Psychiatry*, 121, pp. 241–58.

Buglass, D. and Horton, J. (1974) 'A scale for predicting subsequent suicidal behaviour', *British Journal of Psychiatry*, 124, pp. 573–8.

Butler, A., Oldman, C. and Greve, J. (1983) *Sheltered Housing for the Elderly: Policy, Practice and the Consumer*, London, Allen & Unwin.

Camus, A. (1975) *The Myth of Sisyphus*, Harmondsworth, Penguin.

Caplan, G. (1964) *Principles of Preventive Psychiatry*, London, Tavistock.

Chowdhury, N., Hicks, R.C. and Kreitman, N. (1973) 'Evaluation of an aftercare service for parasuicide (attempted suicide) patients', *Social Psychiatry*, 8, pp. 67–81.

Clare, A. (1976) *Psychiatry in Dissent*, London, Tavistock.

Cooper, B. *et al* (1975) 'Mental health care in the community: an evaluative study', *Psychological Medicine*, 5 (4), pp. 372–80.

Crammer, J., Barraclough, B. and Heine, B. (1978) *The Use of Drugs in Psychiatry*, London, Gaskell.

Creer, C. (1975) 'Social work with patients and their families' in Wing, J.K. (ed.) *Schizophrenia: Towards a New Synthesis*, London, Academic Press.

Curran, D., Partridge, M. and Storey, P. (1975) *Psychological Medicine*, Edinburgh, Churchill Livingstone.

Davies, M. (1981) *The Essential Social Worker: A Guide to Positive Practice*, London, Heinemann.

Edwards, A.H.E. (1976) *Shaw's Guide to Mental Health Services*, London, Shaw & Sons.

Eysenck, H.J. (1975) *The Future of Psychiatry*, London, Methuen.

Fischer, J. and Gochros, H.L. (1975) *Planned Behavioural Change: Behaviour Modification in Social Work*, New York, Free Press.

Gibbons, J. *et al.* (1978) 'Evaluation of a social work service for self-poisoning patients', *British Journal of Psychiatry*, 133 (8), pp. 111–18.

Gibbons, J. *et al.* (1979) 'Clients' reactions to task-centred casework. A follow-up study', *British Journal of Social Work*, 9 (2), pp. 203–16.

Ginsberg, G. and Marks, I.M. (1977) 'Costs and Benefits of Behavioural Psycho-therapy: a pilot study of neurotics treated by nurse-therapists', *Psychological Medicine*, 7, pp. 685–700.

Goffman, E. (1961) *Asylums: Essays on the Social Situation of Mental Patients and Other Inmates*, Harmondsworth, Penguin.

Goldberg, D. and Huxley P. (1980) *Mental Illness in the Community*, London, Tavistock.

Goldberg, E. *et al.* (1977) 'Prediction of relapse in schizophrenic outpatients treated by drugs and socio-therapy', *Archives of General Psychiatry*, 34, pp. 171–84.

Goldstein, E.G. (1974) 'The influence of parental attitudes on psychiatric treatment outcome', *Social Casework*, June, pp. 350–9.

Gostin, L. (1977) *A Human Condition*, London, MIND.

Gostin, L. and Rassaby, E. (1981) *Representing the Mentally Ill and Handicapped*, London, MIND.

Göttfries, I. and Rüdeberg, K. (1981) 'Role of neuroleptics in an integrated treatment programme for chronic schizophrenics', in Göttfries, I., 'Long-term neuroleptic treatment, benefits and risks', pp. 44–52 *Acta Psychiatrica Scandinavica Supplement*, 291, p. 63.

Greenley, J.R. (1979) 'Family symptom tolerance and hospitalisation experience of psychiatric patients', in, Simmons, R.G. (ed.) *Research into Community and Mental Health*, New York, JAI Press, pp. 357–86.

Hamilton, M. (1959) 'The assessment of anxiety states by rating', *British Journal of Psychology*, pp. 50–5.

Hamilton, M. (1960) 'A rating scale for depression', *Journal of Neurology, Neurosurgery and Psychiatry*, pp. 56–61.

Hamilton, M. (ed.) (1978) *Fish's Outline of Psychiatry*, Edinburgh, Wright.

Hawton, K. and Blackstock, E. (1976) 'General Practice aspects of self-poisoning and self-injury', *Psychological Medicine*, 6, p. 571.

Hawton, K. and Roberts, J.C. (1981) 'The association between child abuse and suicide', *British Journal of Social Work*, 11 (4), pp. 415–420.

Hogarty, G.E. *et al.* (1979) 'Fluphenazine and social therapy', *Archives of General Psychiatry*, 36, pp. 1283–1293.

Hoggett, B. (1976) *Mental Health*, London, Sweet & Maxwell.

Holden, U. and Woods, R. (1982) *Reality Orientation*, Edinburgh, Churchill Livingstone.

Holding, T.A. (1974) 'The BBC "Befrienders" series and its effects', *British Journal of Psychiatry*, 124, 470.

Hudson, B.L. (1974) 'The families of agoraphobics treated by behavioural therapy', *British Journal of Social Work*, 4 (1), pp. 51–60. pp. 51–60.

Hudson, B.L. (1982) *Social Work with Psychiatric Patients*, London, Macmillan.

Huxley, P. and Fitzpatrick, R. (1983) 'Probable extent of minor mental illness in adult clients of social workers: a pilot study', *British Journal of Social Work*.

Jehu, D. *et al.* (1972) *Behaviour Modification in Social Work*, Chichester, Wiley.

Jones, K. (1972) *The History of the Mental Health Services*, London, Routledge & Kegan Paul.
Jones, R. (1982) *Encyclopaedia of Social Services Law and Practice*, London, Sweet & Maxwell.
Jones, R.L. and Pritchard, C. (1980) *Social Work with Adolescents*, London, Routledge & Kegan Paul.
Kerfoot, M. (1979) 'Parent—child role reversal and adolescent suicidal behaviour', *Journal of Adolescence*, 2, pp. 337–43.
Kerfoot, M. (1980) 'The family context of adolescent suicidal behaviour', *Journal of Adolescence*, 3, pp. 335–46.
Kreitman, N. (ed.) (1977) *Parasuicide*, London, John Wiley.
Laing, R.D. (1970) *The Divided Self*, Harmondsworth, Penguin.
Laing R.D. (1971) *Self and Others*, Harmondsworth, Penguin.
Lazarus, A.A. (1971) *Behaviour Therapy and Beyond*, New York, McGraw-Hill.
Lazarus, A.A. (1976) *Multi-Modal Behaviour Therapy*, New York, Springer.
Leach, J. and Wing, J.K. (1979) *Helping Destitute Men*, London, Tavistock.
Leon, C.A. and Micklin, M. (1978) 'Who shall be hospitalised? Some social and psychological correlates of alternative dispositions of the mentally ill', *Acta Psychiatrica Scandinavica*, 58, pp. 87–111.
Lidz, T., Cornelison, A.R. and Fleck, S. (1965) *Schizophrenia and the Family*, New York International Universities Press.
Lindberg, D. (1981) 'Management of schizophrenia. Long term clinical studies with special reference to the combination of psychotherapy with depot neuroleptics', *Acta Psychiatrica Scandinavica*, 293, 63.
Lindemann, E (1944) 'The symptomatology and management of acute grief', *American Journal of Psychiatry*, 101, pp. 141–148.
Linford-Rees, W.L. (1970) *A Short Textbook of Psychiatry*, London, Unibooks.
Littlewood, R. and Lipsedge, M. (1982) *Aliens and Alienists: Ethnic Minorities and Psychiatry*, Harmondsworth, Penguin.
Marks, I. (1975) in Hersen, R. (ed.) *Progress in Behaviour Modification*, London, Academic Press.
Moreno, J. (1934) *Who Shall Survive?*, New York, Beacon Books.
Olsen, R.M. (ed.) (1979) *The Care of the Mentally Disordered: an Examination of some Alternatives to Hospital Care*, Birmingham, BASW.
Olsen, Rolf, (1981) 'Untrained and unsafe', *Social Work Today*, 13, 10, p. 1.
Olsen, R.M. (1982) 'A qualified success', *Community Care*, December, 23/30, pp. 19–20.
Parkes, C.M. (1975) *Bereavement: Studies of Grief in Adult Life*, Harmondsworth, Penguin.
Paykel, E.S., Prussoff, B.A. and Myers, J.K. (1975) 'Suicide attempts and recent life events – a controlled comparison', *Archives of General Psychiatry*, 32 (3), pp. 327–33.

Perls, F. (1973) *The Gestalt Approach*: *Eye Witness to Therapy*, New York, Science and Behaviour Books.

Pinker, R.A. (1982) 'An alternative view', pp. 236–262, Barclay Report, *Social Workers: Their Role and Tasks*, London, Bedford Square Press.

Prins, H. (1980) *Offenders, Deviants, or Patients?*, London, Tavistock.

Pritchard, C. and Butler, A. (1976) 'Why Specialism? The case for mental health social work', *Social Work Today*, 7(6), pp. 176–90.

Pritchard, C. and King, R. (1980) 'Changes in the mutual perceptions of trainee GPs and social work students', *Social Work Service*, 24, pp. 47–52.

Pritchard, C. and Cunliffe, A. (1983) 'A positive strategy for community based mental health', *Social Policy and Administration* (in press).

Pritlove, J.H. (1976) 'Evaluating a group home: problems and results', *British Journal of Social Work*, 6 (3), pp. 353–376.

Ramon, S., Bancroft, J.H.J. and Skrimshire, A.M. (1975) 'Attitudes towards self-poisoning among physicians and nurses in a general hospital', *British Journal of Psychiatry*, 127, pp. 257–264.

Reid, W. and Epstein, L. (1972) *Task Centred Casework*, New York, Columbia University Press.

Rogers, C. (1961) *On Becoming A Person*, Boston, Houghton Mifflin.

Rush, A.J. *et al* (1977) 'Comparative efficacy of cognitive-therapy and pharmaco-therapy in the treatment of depressed outpatients', *Cognitive Therapy Research*, 1, pp. 17–37.

Sainsbury, P. (1955) *Suicide in London*, London, Chapman & Hall.

Sandler, J., Dare, C. and Holder, A. (1973) *The Patient and the Analyst*, London, Allen & Unwin.

Sartre, Jean-Paul (1969) *Being and Nothingness*, London, Methuen.

Scheff, T. (1966) *Being Mentally Ill*, London, Weidenfeld & Nicolson.

Schneider, K. (1959) *Clinical Psychopathology* (trans Hamilton, M.W.), New York, Grune & Stratton.

Sedgwick, P. (1982) *PsychoPolitics*, London, Pluto.

Seligman, M.E.P. (1975) *Helplessness*: *On Depression, Development and Death*, San Francisco, Freeman.

Shepherd, D.M. and Barraclough, B.M. (1979) 'Help for those bereaved by suicide', *British Journal of Social Work*, 9, 1.

Siassi, I. (1979) 'A comparison of open-ended psychoanalytically-oriented psychotherapy with other therapies', *Journal of Clinical Psychiatry*, 40 (1), pp. 25–32.

Siegler, M. and Osmond, H. (1966) 'Models of madness', *British Journal of Psychiatry*, 112, pp. 1193–1203.

Skynner, A.C.R. (1976) *One Flesh, Separate Persons. Principles of Family and Marital Psychotherapy*, London, Constable.

Smith, A.C. (1982) *Schizophrenia and Madness*, London, Allen & Unwin.

Smith, C.R. (1982) *Social Work with the Dying and Bereaved*, London, Macmillan.

Snaith, R.P. *et al.* (1978) 'A clinical scale for the self-assessment of irritability', *British Journal of Psychiatry*, 132, pp. 164–171.

Stein, L. and Test, M.A. (1980) 'Alternatives to mental hospital treatment', *Archives of General Psychiatry*, 37, pp. 392–7.

Stevenson, O. and Parsloe, P. (1978) *Social Service Teams: The Practitioners' View*, London, DHSS, HMSO.

Stoffelmayr, B.E. *et al.* (1979) 'Maintenance of staff behaviour', *Behavioural Research and Therapy*, 17 (3), pp. 271–3.

Szasz, T. (1960) 'The myth of mental illness', *American Psychologist*, 15 February pp. 113–18.

Szmukler, G.I. *et al.* (1981) 'Compulsory admissions Parts I and II', *Psychological Medicine* 11 pp. 617–36, 825–38.

Trethowan, W.H. (1975), 'Pills for personal problems', *British Medical Journal*, 3, pp. 749–51.

Trower, P., Bryant, B. and Argyle, M. (1978) *Social Skills and Mental Health*, London, Methuen.

Truax, C.B. and Carkhuff, R.R. (1967) *Toward Effective Counselling and Psychotherapy: Training and Practice*, Chicago, Aldine.

Vaughn, C.E. and Leff, J.P. (1976) 'The influence of the family and social factors on the course of psychiatric illness', *British Journal of Psychiatry*, 129, pp. 125–37.

Vigderhaus, G. and Fishman, G. (1978) 'The impact of unemployment on family integration and on changing suicide rates in the USA 1920–1969', *Social Psychiatry*, 13, 4, pp. 239–48.

Waldrond-Skinner, S. (1976) *Family Therapy — the Treatment of Natural Systems*, London, Routledge & Kegan Paul.

Wansbrough, S.N. and Cooper, P. (1980) *Open Employment after Mental Illness*, London, Tavistock.

Weisbrod, B.A. *et al.* (1980) 'Alternatives to mental hospital treatment: economic cost–benefit analysis', *Archives of General Psychiatry*, 30, pp. 771–8.

Weissman, M.M. (1974) 'Treatment effect on the social adjustment of depressed people', *Archives of General Psychiatry*, 30, pp. 771–8.

Weissman, M.M. *et al.* (1981) 'Depressed outpatients results after one year treatment with drugs and/or inter-personal psychotherapy', *Archives of General Psychiatry*, 37, pp. 400–5.

Wing, J.K. (ed.) (1975) *Schizophrenia From Within*, Surbiton, Surrey, National Schizophrenia Fellowship.

Wing, J.K. (1978) *Reasoning about Madness*, Oxford University Press.

Wing, J.K. and Brown, G.W. (1970) *Institutionalism and Schizophrenia*, Cambridge University Press.

Wynne, L., Ryckoff, I., Day, J. and Hirsch, S. (1958) 'Pseudo-mutuality in the family relations of schizophrenics', *Psychiatry*, 21, pp. 205–20.

Yalom, I.D. (1970) *The Theory and Practice of Group Psychotherapy*, New York, Basic Books.

Index